CURRENCY
R I S K
Management

A Handbook for Financial Managers, Brokers, and Their Consultants

Gary Shoup

Glenlake Publishing Company, Ltd.
Chicago • London • New Delhi

AMACOM
American Management Association
New York • Atlanta • Boston • Chicago • Kansas City • San Francisco • Washington, D.C.
Brussels • Mexico City • Tokyo • Toronto

© 1998 Center for Futures Education, Inc.

NkP

ISBN: 0-8144-0439-1

Printed in the United States of America.

AMACOM

American Management Association
1601 Broadway
New York, New York 10019
Visit the American Management Association and AMACOM on-line at
http:\\www.amanet.org

Table of Contents

iii

Acknowledgments

This book was made possible by an extensive review of the works by many writers, educators, and practitioners who are accomplished in this field. To them I owe my gratitude. I also wish to thank John Walsh and Donna Greenlee, whose ongoing encouragement and support contributed mightily to this effort in many ways. Much of the information in Chapter Seven is derived from research by John Walsh in the area of futures' sales techniques.

I am grateful to David Zischke and Manish Jain of the International Business Development Center at Michigan State University, Eli Broad School of Business, as well as Dr. Kai Sorensen, for their ideas and suggestions, of which many are found in this book.

Finally, I especially wish to thank Chalouy Shoup. Her long-standing, active support and assistance in this project was crucial from beginning to end. Of course, the errors found herein belong to me.

Gary Shoup

About the Author

Gary Shoup, author, lecturer, and commodity trading advisor, is an authority on the subject of foreign exchange, and a pioneer in foreign currency management. As a former Merrill Lynch broker and futures specialist, Mr. Shoup established a clientele ranging from individuals to Fortune 100 corporations. He introduced hedging strategies to corporate managers at a time when the concept was virtually unknown outside the agricultural community. Working in conjunction with his firm's international bank, he was among the first to combine interbank and exchange features in currency hedging programs.

As this book demonstrates, Mr. Shoup skillfully imparts highly technical information in a breezy, often humorous, always easy-to-follow style. His sales experience comes to the foreground in the last chapter. Here he discusses techniques for presenting a risk management program to corporate decision makers. Unless the principals of currency hedging can be successfully communicated, they will not be implemented. For this reason, his sales concepts are crucial to the success of the risk management program.

Preface

In preparation of this new edition, I was asked to review the contents and make changes where warranted. Certain changes have been made for the sake of clarity, and to correct the inevitable typo that seems to escape the closest scrutiny. There are new exhibits, and some of the originals have been given a new appearance, again for the sake of clarity.

It is encouraging to note, however, that the text is as current today as when first written three years ago. The underlying concepts and case studies are just as valid; in fact, even more so. The risk of currency exposure is more evident today, and the proposed solutions more urgently needed. Indeed, the only major change in the last few years involves the *scope* of currency risk. When this book first appeared, currency risk was a growing, but still largely unrecognized, financial problem at the corporate level. Today currency risk is recognized not only as a financial problem, but as a social issue of the times, one capable of wrecking havoc wave-like around the world. Today, the concept of exposure is not just about corporate assets and liabilities, but about sovereign debt, political stability and economic well-being.

Four developments in the last few years promise to have a lasting effect on currency risk management. These are:

1. the unrelenting strength of the U.S. dollar as it becomes the world's store house of value;

2. the collapse of the pegged currency regime in Asia and elsewhere;

3. the approaching European unified currency; and

4. the growing regulatory movement toward more transparency in the accounting of derivatives, including currency derivatives.

The Indefatigable U.S. Dollar

Figure 1-1 (on page 13) illustrates the major uptrend of the U.S. dollar over the last three years. The historic effect of an appreciating currency is a weakening competitive position for domestic companies whose costs of production are denominated in that particular currency. One classic study, reviewed elsewhere in this book, is that of Chrysler, and the significant share of the domestic market it lost to the Japanese automobile industry beginning in the late 1970s.

Today the adverse effects of this operating exposure for American business appear more muted, perhaps because today America is a more competitive producer. The orientation is more toward production and less toward consumption. Companies that produce in dollars and sell in foreign currency are more aware than ever of the unrelenting competition "out there." They are holding their price and either managing their exposures or managing to live with thinner margins. In either case, they are experiencing greater challenges as a result of their operating and strategic exposures. Producers that still invoice their foreign trade accounts in U.S. dollars for price-driven products are fast becoming non-competitive. At the same time, international purchasing managers are able to drive much harder bargains with their suppliers. Those who are adept at currency management, however, know it is advisable to help their less sophisticated suppliers manage their own foreign currency exposures. When a supplier become insolvent and disappears, the effect can be as damaging as losing a key customer.

How did the U.S. dollar come to be the world's monetary powerhouse? Reuters reports that in the month of January, 1998, *"the inflation rate is at it's lowest point in a generation., industrial output continues to rise, consumer confidence remains solid and economic growth, at 3.8 percent last year, has not been stronger since Ronald Regan was President."*[1] This convergence of events creates a highly stable currency environment, and stability is the one area where most of the world's currencies fall short. Fiat currencies are notorious for their inability to perform reliably as a store of value, which is a key role of any serious currency. Historically, gold filled that void. Today, the dollar does the job just as credibly, and flights to quality now end up less in precious metal vaults and more in a booming U.S. stock market or in U.S. treasuries. Of course, nothing goes up forever, and the dollar will again top out, losing value against other major currencies. As of this writing, however, the U.S. dollar continues to look as "good as gold."

The Put-Upon Pegged Currency

Until July 2nd, 1997, the Thai Baht was pegged to a basket that included the U.S. dollar, the yen, Deutsche mark, the rupiah and other currencies. For all practical purposes, however, the U.S. dollar was the primary currency of the basket, and the baht was the equivalent of a U.S. four cent piece, albeit given to narrow price fluctuations from day to day. As a significant trading partner and long-time buyer of U.S. military hardware, there were strong political and economic reasons to maintain a predictable relationship between the dollar and the baht.

In recent years, excess investment capital from Europe, the United States and Japan sought out regions that could offer both high growth potential and monetary stability. Thailand, high on the list, was soon in the midst of an economic boom of historic proportions. This period ended abruptly in May, 1997, with the baht under heavy speculative attack. On July 2nd, The Bank of Thailand abandoned the peg, and the baht sharply depreciated, falling eventually to below two cents in value. Following like dominos, the Indonesian rupiah, the Malaysian ringett, and the Korean won also fell to significantly lower values, their pegs abandoned in every case. Even the neighboring currencies of Hong Kong and Singapore were shaken. In the aftermath, a disastrous financial crisis enveloped the region. In Indonesia, the economy came to a virtual stand still for a time, resulting in social unrest. The chaos was not confined to Asia, but swept up financial markets around the world. As of this writing, the final curtain has yet to fall on this still-unfolding drama.

What went wrong? Our discussion of real versus nominal exchange rates in Chapter Three indicates an inherent instability of the pegged currency regime. The problem begins with a sudden influx of portfolio investment capital. In contrast to foreign direct investment, short-term investment funds translate into short-term foreign debt. In addition, foreign investment capital flowing into an economy causes the monetary base to grow as bank loans proliferate, thereby fueling domestic inflation. Since the nominal exchange rate can not change to compensate for this change of monetary condition, the currency becomes overvalued in real terms. Interest rates rise, creating arbitrage opportunities in which banks borrow low-cost reserve currencies and convert them into high-cost local currencies. These in turn are loaned out in increasing amounts and decreasing due diligence to fuel the booming economy. In addition, should the policies of the central bank be somewhat murky, should the fiscal condition of the banking sector be less than transparent, should the financial system be weak, the currency is undermined and vulnerable to attack, regardless of which regime it is in.

The IMF estimates that more than $100 billion is currently available in hedge funds, speculative mutual funds, and proprietary trading accounts.[2] Since most of this money can be leveraged between five- to ten-times, it is more than enough to test the staying power of a fair-size central bank. In Thailand, as the baht became more overvalued, it became more vulnerable to speculative attack. When the Thai central bank buckled under the ensuing selling pressure, panic swept over financial districts throughout the region, as other currencies suddenly appeared vulnerable to the same fate. Throughout the region, banking and commercial interests with short-term dollar liabilities rushed into the market to cover their short positions. By doing so, they launched a much more devastating attack on their currency than the speculators were capable of doing enmasse. Indeed, the precise role the speculator in the ensuing conflagration has yet to be determined.

The short trader is recognized by his nervous propensity to jump and run at the slightest hint of trouble. This is because of the virtually unlimited risk inherent in a short position. Sharp, major market moves, such as witnessed in the Asian currency markets, are the hallmark of desperate shorts trying to get out and stay solvent, rather than hopeful longs trying to get in and get rich.

The lesson for the currency manager is self-evident:

> "Fiat currencies play dual roles. They're used as legal tender, exchanged for things of real value, and invested, but they also serve as a statement of policy. The German Deutsche mark of the 1990s and the Reichs mark of the 1920s both have played the role in Germany of a medium of exchange, but are vastly different statements of policy. Accepting currency in payment of debts is an act of legality required by legal tender laws. Accepting a <u>particular amount</u> of currency as payment is an act of confidence, both in the central bank and in the politicians of the country."[3]

Foreign exchange risk comes in many guises, including credit, market, liquidity, settlement, political and legal risks. We are learning anew that the currency manager must become familiar with all of them, scrutinize them, and take nothing for granted.

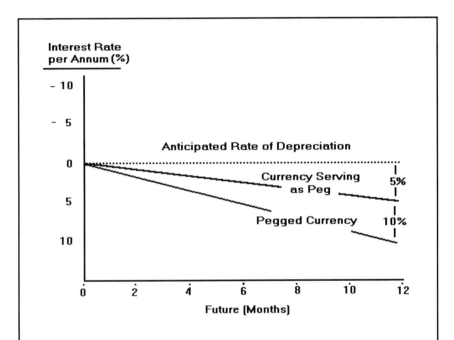

Diverging interest rates between pegged currencies and their related reserve currency should be carefully scrutinized. These often indicate changes in the real rate of exchange that can not be compensated by changes in the nominal rate of exchange, which remains fixed. As a result, the central bank comes under increasing pressure to defend the peg from speculative attack.

The Euro; Dawn of a New Age

On January 1st, 1999, the "euro" is slated to make its debut. Although less than one year away, as of this writing, controversy as to the timing, and even the wisdom, of a European unified currency continues to swirl over the continent. If momentum carries the day, however, on this date member states of the Economic and Monetary Union (EMU) will convert their currencies into euros at a rate based on their separate weights in the ecu currency basket. For the following three years, the national currency of each EMU member and the euro will be interchangeable. It is anticipated that during this period the euro will be used mainly in the financial markets, interbank transfers, international payments and commercial transactions. The public will continue to transact at the retail level in the notes and coins of the national currency. Then, on January 1st, 2002, the notes and coins of the individual countries will be called in and exchanged for euro notes and coins, the new legal tender of the EMU. European countries that are not EMU members may choose to remain in a made-over Exchange Rate Mechanism, known as ERM II, with the euro serving as the anchor currency.

If indeed the sun should rise on this new era, only time will tell whether the the euro will succeed as a strong currency, vying for reserve status with the U.S. dollar, or soon become another ecu fading from view. The advantages of the euro cited by its proponents are exchange rate stability, reserve currency status, elimination of foreign exchange costs, transparent markets and structurally lower interest rates due to the fiscal restraints of member countries.

The disadvantages, which, according to skeptics, are virtually insurmountable, are the austerity measures required by all members, regardless of national economic conditions, and the surrender of monetary policy as an economic lever and funding source for social and political programs. Not only the money supply, but interest rates as well, will slip away from national control.

Between January 1st, 1999 and January 1st, 2002, the currency manager will have to contend with a duel currency system in every EMU country in which his company does business. Assuming the introduction of the euro is not derailed, certain steps should be taken well in advance of what promises to be a trying period. The following projects should be considered:

1. Form a task force to coordinate the company's response to the euro.

2. Gather information as details unfold. For example, conversion will occur based on ecu basket rates as of December 31st, 1998. Foreign exchange gains and losses will be realized at that rate.

3. Analyze both the opportunities and risks of the euro's effect on sales, manufacturing, procurement, engineering, finance and administration. What will be the effect on international operations?

Intracompany transactions? Wages? Pensions? How will the competition be effected?

4. Bring in outside sources early, such as the accountant, loan officer, software supplier. Determine the role of each in the transition.

5. Retail operations in EMU countries will require a great deal of lead time to prepare for the transition period. Beginning January 1st, 2002, the public will be able to transact in either currency for a period of time. This will require duel price labeling, publishing and accounting for shelf items, inventory and services.

The euro is a bold experiment. Much is at stake. If things work as planned, Europe will stand head-to-head with the United States as a financial superpower. Whatever the outcome, the transition will test the resolve of politicians and citizens alike as social and economic goals converge, and a new culture is forged.

FASB Moves Toward Greater Transparency

From its headquarters in Norwalk, Connecticut, the Financial Accounting Standards Board (FASB) fired a shot across the bow of the derivatives industry on June 20, 1996. It took the form of an exposure draft for a proposed statement entitled, "Accounting for Derivative and Similar Financial Instruments and for Hedging Activities." The objective is to make corporate derivative trading for hedging purposes more transparent to the outside world. As of now, the new standard is to take effect for fiscal years after June 15, 1999. However, both supporting and opposing forces to the proposal are weighing in, and the outcome is still uncertain.

Should the statement be adopted, many derivative instruments now carried off-balance sheet, such as options, forwards, futures and swaps, will become balance sheet assets and liabilities measured at fair (market) value. In essence, the profits and losses from derivative trading, be it for hedging or speculation, will be posted in real time for all to see.

FASB 52, the current standard for foreign currency exposure, allows hedging results for transaction exposures to be "deferred," along with value changes in the exposure itself. (See Chapter Five.) The proposed standard amends FASB 52 by providing hedge accounting for cash flow exposure, which was previously disallowed. This is a welcome and long-awaited development in the field of currency risk management. After all, transaction exposure and cash flow exposure are simply two sides of the same coin.

In the spirit of give and take, however, the method of hedge accounting itself will change. Value changes of derivatives used for hedges will be reported (not deferred) for each period, along with the offsetting values of the exposure. Hedge gains and losses not offset due to hedging inefficiencies go directly to earnings, which certainly will encourage the advent of more efficient hedging. There are also important changes in the criteria necessary to allow hedge accounting, the most notable being the increased scrutiny given to the underlying hedge program. In other words, not only gains or losses, but the strategy that created them, will become more visible.

Regardless of the final deposition of the proposal, the trend toward more accountability in the area of derivatives is unmistakable. Therefore, the ability to *fashion*, *present* and *explain* the an effective, currency risk management program has never been more essential.

I hope the information in this book provides you with the means to perfect that ability.

Introduction

Life down on the farm has changed for good. Drive down any rural byway and you'll spot almost as many roof-top satellite dishes as silos. With data links to Chicago and New York, real-time price moves for cotton, corn, and cattle blink across monitor screens nestled in homes among the hills and valleys. Farmers today keep one weather eye on the sky and another on digital data flow. They're able to react at once to the fluctuations of a world market place.

Embracing this new technology was not easy. Fifteen years ago, it was rare to find a farmer marketing his products through Chicago from an office, for example, somewhere in Iowa. Agricultural products then were marketed the way they always had been. When the corn came in from the field, or when the fat cattle came out of feed lots, the farmer trucked his goods to the nearest elevator or auction barn to sell for whatever they would bring. Of course, all his neighbors were there. Together, they would finish selling the entire output from a year's worth of interest and labor in two or three weeks. With a buyer's market trying to absorb the harvest glut, the prices paid would often set new lows. Like clockwork, the producer traditionally sold every year at the bottom third of the price range. This pattern was so predictable that speculators consistently bought agricultural futures during harvest time to profit from the seasonal low of the cycle.

In the late 1970s, inflation and futures trading took off together, and I joined in as a commodity broker. I discovered that my natural bent was more toward educating than speculating, so I headed into the countryside to "teach those farmers a thing or two." With a copy of the *Wall Street Journal* and a set of basis charts, I began knocking on doors. If invited in,

1

I would spread my wares on the kitchen table and, within a half hour, explain all about hedging with futures. Scribing in the air with my arms, I would illustrate with a flourish how my listener could greatly enhance his future. After all, I would add, hedging farm products is simply playing by the speculator's rules and they're the ones making the money.

The typical reaction was discouraging. After I told the farmer my story, he would tell me his. "Not a gambler," he would say, or "how about that fellow up the road who lost his farm hedging commodities?" I heard about the truck load of eggs dumped in some poor trader's front yard overnight because he overstayed a position. (Remember trading eggs?) I heard about the commodity broker who took "that one fellow" to the cleaners' and then ran off with his wife.

Perhaps as disheartening were the success stories I heard. It was never a personal experience; usually it was about a neighbor who locked in the very top dime of the market. "Won big," the prospect would whisper, casting a wary eye around the coffee shop. "Can you do that well?"

Although I "educated" many farmers, only a few opened hedge accounts. Fewer still actually traded them. I was convinced I would stir up more interest if I were making book on next year's crop instead of trying to hedge it. I was not alone. Most brokers I talked with at the time were experiencing the same thing. We were amazed at the resistance to a management tool of such obvious benefit.

We now know, looking back, that the reaction could not have been otherwise. The concept of risk management is not absorbed in thirty minutes over a kitchen table. Management advice coming from a stranger unaware of the farmer's personal operation was all too easy to dismiss. We learned that the educational process involves a two-way relationship. To be successful, brokers in the commercial end of the futures business need to know their clients' businesses inside out. They must become business advisors, not just brokers.

Today, risk management is much more sophisticated, and the educational process is keeping pace. More hedging tools are available for fine-tuning individual operations. Now, most large farm operators would not consider going into a planting season without a hedge program firmly in place. An increasing number of loan officers insist on it; however, even in this sector, risk management is not at all universal. A good deal of anecdotal evidence suggests that a lot of farmers who do not hedge would do so if they only understood it better. Still, today a great many farmers could teach a great many of us brokers a thing or two about risk management.

We have come a long way from our agricultural roots. Raw materials and commodities of all types can now be price managed through the tools available. It has reached a point where, for example, a refiner can buy crude oil, crack it into products, sell the heating oil and retain the gasoline, all with a keyboard, a monitor, and a modem. Producers and users of copper, nickel, aluminum, lumber, and gold can lock in cost and revenue the same way a farmer can lock in the price of wheat, cotton, diammonium phosphate and hogs.

The most exciting growth is in the area of financial products. There is, of course, the image problem. Farmers really did lose the farm in the futures markets. There is plenty of blame to go around, and we have to own up to our part of it. We watched, profitably, as the farmer went from locking up his selling price on one end to locking up his replacement costs on the other end, then his input costs in the middle, and finally (to hedge against inflation, you understand) a few contracts of silver to boot. What started out as a conservative hedging strategy often ended up as outright gambling. Unwary users suffered heavy losses, especially during the 1980s when the raging bull market suddenly began its long descent.

The engineers of financial futures distanced themselves from such goings-on in the agricultural market place. The phrase "commodities trading" with its negative connotation, was replaced with "futures trading." After all, they sniffed, stocks, bonds, and currencies are really a breed apart from pork bellies and soybeans. Then program trading with index futures became implicated in the 1987 stock market collapse. Almost immediately, this term also began to fall into disfavor. We turned to a neutral, sophisticated sounding term. One that was not implicated in unsavory goings-on. One that had a nice ring to it—*derivatives.*

We've gone full circle. Today, instead of mentioning the now-dreaded "D" word, we're back to referring to financial instruments as exchange-traded futures, over-the-counter options, options on futures, interbank forwards, and counter-party agreements. "Financial futures" are in vogue again.

They were formally introduced to the public in 1972 by the Chicago Mercantile Exchange in the form of a contract for 125,000 Swiss francs. (Banks were dealing in forwards long before that, but few people knew of it.) Currency and interest rate futures came of age about the time commodity futures peaked, and virtually exploded in popularity during the 1980s. They are still growing. Outstanding bank balances in exchange-traded derivatives jumped from $583 billion in 1986 to $8.8 trillion by the end of 1994. The demand is not confined to exchange-traded instruments. Trading in over-the-counter derivatives grew even faster, from $500 billion in 1986 to an estimated $10.2 trillion by the end of 1994.[1]

The different products now available permit us to manage the price risk in foreign currencies, equity portfolios, bond portfolios, and money markets both domestically and overseas. Selecting from the tools now at hand, a corporate treasurer can literally construct his own exchange rate and yield for any major country, either locking it in, swapping it, letting it float, or anything in between.

With the advent of financial futures, we brokers (now "risk management consultants") re-armed ourselves with charts, tables, printouts, and literature. Again we sallied forth—not into farm kitchens this time, but into conference rooms. Education began anew, but the response is no different. There is a familiar ring to it. "We manufacture products; we don't gamble in currencies."

The solution, of course, is the same as before. If we want to be providers of foreign currency management, we must begin by educating ourselves. We must understand our clients' businesses, and know how they relate to such things as off-balance sheet hedging, FASB 52 conventions, counter-party credit risk, translation versus transactional exposure, visible versus hidden exposure, and all the rest. Finally, we must be able to present the currency management program to whoever stamps the account forms for final approval.

Currency risk management is where agricultural hedging was fifteen years ago; however, there is a new wrinkle. American business cannot afford a ten- to fifteen-year learning curve. In many cases, company growth (in some cases, company solvency) depends on risk management becoming corporate policy *tomorrow.*

It is difficult to overstate the case. The stakes are enormous. Willingly or not, U.S. commerce is being carried out in a dynamic economy on a global stage. Increasingly, companies of all sizes are exporting, importing, or competing with someone who does. Corporations now routinely arrange financing in overseas capital markets. Portfolio managers, as a matter of course, today look overseas for new investment opportunities.

The trend toward a global economy is unmistakable, accelerating, and probably irreversible. We are witnessing the launching of the third wave, called the World Trade Organization.

International activity does not occur without currency exchange. Every contract or transaction that crosses currency borders results in exposure to foreign exchange risk. John F. Sandner, chairman of the Chicago Mercantile Exchange, addressed this subject during an interview with *Futures Industry*.[2] His remarks refer to price-risk management in general, and exchange-traded derivatives in particular, but, with the international currency markets now exchanging more than one trillion dollars a day, they are very appropriate here:

> "The biggest growth industry in this country, maybe the world, is managing risk. If you can't manage risk, there's going to be a tremendous cost to taking this risk which will be passed on to the consumer...Today, [risk management] is commonplace. If you're a corporate treasurer or have assumed some type of fiduciary responsibility, if you haven't considered futures and options for risk and asset management purposes, you had better be able to explain why not."

This handbook is for bank representatives, futures brokers, securities brokers, cash management consultants, and other providers of financial services who are interested in increasing their business in this exciting area. Our purpose is to help you *develop* and *present* a foreign currency management program. The best-developed program in the world is wasted effort if it doesn't pass muster with the decision makers of the client corporation. In my experience, senior managers and board members appear to be singularly unimpressed with bells and whistles. They are becoming more so, as they watch the financial industry's complex derivative packages unravel. They tend to be "bottom line" people who favor well-tailored programs based on solid, easy-to-understand concepts. This manual is designed to help you develop and present just such a program.

CHAPTER 1

An Overview*

We once lived in an isolated country; American business cut its teeth on domestic consumption. When we did go overseas, we often monopolized the field, be it in soybeans, computers, chemicals, or airplanes. We worried about only one currency: the U.S. dollar. To our advantage, this currency is still the world's leading reserve, the one most in demand as a store of value and as an invoice currency. Most world trade is still denominated in dollars; petrodollars in the middle east; Eurodollars the world over. Trading from this position of strength, corporate America was largely able to avoid exchange rate risk. Today, the tactic still most often employed in the United States for dealing with foreign currency risk is simply not to deal in foreign currency.

According to a study of 12,000 U.S. corporations filing with the SEC, less than 10% made any mention of foreign exchange in their reports.[1] Other studies confirm this non-involvement in foreign exchange. A survey by the Philadelphia Stock Exchange indicates that only about 30% of all U.S. managers hedge risk of *any* kind. In contrast, less than 40% of European managers do *not* hedge risk.[2] These figures illustrate the provincial nature of American commerce. Europeans, unlike Americans, have a long tradition of cross-border trading. They are aware of the dynamics of currency exchange rates and know how to deal with them, often to their advantage. In fact, it's quite common for French companies to set up in-house cost centers having all the earmarks of an international banking operation. Many commercial entities in France seem to thrive on currency exposure, and manage it with as much enthusiasm as they do other segments of the business.

They are not alone. Today, London is the world's leading financial center for foreign exchange, having taken that position from New York by default. Japanese traders traditionally look at foreign exchange exposure from a strategic point of view as inherent in the sale. They recognize the opportunity it affords. They often *assume* the currency risk, always *account* for it, and usually *manage* it to their advantage.

The dollar may still be king, but its crown is slipping. The fact that the attempt to avoid foreign exchange risk is exacting a heavy toll on U.S. commerce can no longer be seriously disputed. Today, U.S. dollar-denominated bids on overseas projects—the same projects for which European and Japanese competitors bid in local currency—are not nearly as successful as they once were. The global business environment has become much more competitive. Gaining market share today often means direct investment in assembly shops, inventory, advertising, and other expenses all requiring local currency. Today, overseas customers demand price sheets and catalogs denominated in *their* currency, not ours. Letters of credit invoiced in U.S. dollars, payable upon shipment in, say, 90 days, are becoming too risky to foreign buyers. The volatility of the currency markets is too great. For years, U.S. companies submitted U.S. dollar invoices to overseas customers who were left to grapple with the exchange inherent in the invoices. Today, however, there are numerous competitors in the wings who are eager to assume that risk for their customers.

Corporate managers just now are awaking to the fact that refusing to deal with exposure risk does not make it disappear; it merely transfers the risk to the customer (or, when sourcing abroad, to the supplier). As far as a long-term business relationship goes, it doesn't really matter which party carries the exposure on the books. Left unmanaged, the eventual fallout affects buyer and seller alike.

This point was illustrated during a recent seminar sponsored by the U.S Department of Commerce to promote export business. One of the speakers was the export manager for a mid-sized industrial fastener manufacturer. He began by relating the ground rules by which his company approaches international marketing, one being that it transacts only in U.S. dollars. Midway through the presentation, he made the point that no company should get involved in exporting unless it's for the long haul. To support his argument, he told about the trials his company experienced during its attempt to market its product line in the United Kingdom. It took several years of effort at great expense and with numerous set-backs, but eventually they prevailed and established themselves as the number two supplier in the UK.

Not long after the company's market was established, the British pound started dropping in value against the dollar, which "was driving us crazy." Their major competitor, a European company, continually undercut them. When asked how they handled that, the speaker replied, "well, we just couldn't compete, so we had to back away from England." It turned out that the European firm could well afford to price them out of the market. Its own foreign operations were doing consistently well, with the company hedging its currency exposures whenever the opportunity arose.

This illustrates the amorphous nature of foreign currency exposure. It crops up in unexpected places. As this export manager discovered, the exposure risk was not confined to a specific asset or liability, but involved an entire market. In some cases, the entire business can be at risk while management remains blissfully unaware of any exposure at all. Examples abound. They crop up whenever brokers gather in corners to exchange war stories. As one strives to outdo the other, someone always comes up with the question, "have you heard about Laker Air?"[3]

Laker Air, a British air charter company, enjoyed a robust business in the 1970s. It captured a market niche by providing travel service to British vacationers flying to the United States. It was quite popular, then, to plan itineraries around overseas shopping trips to New York. With strong pounds in their pockets, compared to the dollar, British citizens could buy consumer goods in the United States at a hefty discount to what they would pay in London. The savings often paid for the air fare and, consequently, flights to New York and back were booked solidly weeks in advance.

Business was so good, in fact, that Laker Air placed orders for five additional DC-10s. Suddenly, things took a dramatic turn. The British pound topped out early in 1981. From $2.40, it dropped sharply to $1.90, continued downward for the next five years, and finally bottomed in 1985 around $1.10. From the perspective of the British traveler, however, the pound wasn't dropping as much as the dollar was soaring. Discounts in New York disappeared and Mediterranean vacations became more alluring. Laker Air started flying a lot of empty seats across the Atlantic.

The swift decline in revenues was not the only difficulty facing Laker Air. Its outstanding dollar-denominated loans for the new airplanes resulted in increasing pound liabilities at the same time its pound revenues were decreasing. The dollar balances remained the same, but it was taking ever more pounds to pay them. The result, of course, was bank-ruptcy.

It is increasingly difficult to sort out the exposures a business might face. As the global economy becomes more interwoven, it becomes more complex. It is not always easy to know which currency affects which product. A company does not have to buy or sell internationally to be exposed to foreign currency risk. This fact has been brought home to a number of U.S. corporations, none more so than to Chrysler Corporation.

Throughout most of the 1960s and 1970s, Chrysler was involved in extensive overseas operations. Beginning in 1977, however, it became mired in red ink and without sufficient reserves to maintain its international presence. A decision was made to retrench, and to concentrate in North America. To implement this strategy, the company sold off its investments in Latin America, Europe, and Australia.

After downsizing, Chrysler focused entirely on the domestic front. It sourced its parts from U.S. suppliers, assembled them in Michigan, and sold the finished products to America. It became the quintessential domestic manufacturer, almost totally submerged in a dollar-denominated economy; however, as it was reorganizing, Toyota and other Japanese car companies began to unload their exports on California docks. Approximately 60% of the cost of these cars was denominated in yen, at an exchange rate of 200 to the dollar and rising. With a cost of goods denominated in a relatively under-valued currency, manufacturing costs were much lower in dollar terms. The Japanese priced the window stickers in dollars accordingly.

Still reeling from skyrocketing oil price increases, American consumers welcomed the economies of these new imports, including their attractive sticker prices. The Japanese carmakers poured their brand new dollar revenues into war chests to be used to capture an even greater share of the U.S. market. Chrysler, at a major cost disadvantage, could only stand aside and watch its market share disappear.

It is interesting to note that Chrysler had no foreign currency exposure on the books. Its assets and liabilities were denominated solely in dollars. Yet the dollar value of the Japanese yen was a definite factor in the fire sale of Chrysler stock to skittish buyers at six dollars a share. Currency exposure involves currency mismatches, and Chrysler certainly had a mismatch on its hands. This exposure surfaced in two areas; first, on the competitors' income statements that made enjoyable reading in Tokyo, and secondly, in Hometown, USA, where yen cost-based cars were replacing dollar cost-based cars in many garages.

Nothing is forever. Beginning in 1989, the yen/dollar exposure started turning the losses of the 1980s into the profits of the 1990s. The yen, at 100 to the dollar, was becoming rather precious. The upsurge in domestic automobile sales at the expense of the Japanese models is one result. As we will see, there are a number of ways to manage currency exposure. Toyota, Honda, Mitsubishi, and others, demonstrating one method, brought over the tooling and set up manufacturing facilities in the United States.

The Various Exposures

The above examples make it quite clear that foreign currency exposure means different things to different companies. Lumping all exposures together as "currency mismatches" does not go far enough. We must ask where the mismatch occurs and how it expresses itself within the corporation. In order to get a handle on it, we must distinguish one type of exposure from another.

This is done with a variety of labels. We hear of translation exposure, transactional exposure, balance sheet exposure, economic exposure, and so forth. One label is as good as another, but for our purposes, let's classify four types of exposures, each managed from a particular perspective and for a particular objective. These classifications, from the narrowest to the broadest, are as follows:

- *Accounting exposure*—This is restricted to contractual exposure. Foreign exchange impacts items on the financial reports. Such items include receivables, payables, and other long- and short-term assets and liabilities. Accounting exposure, having been contracted, is reportable, and therefore highly visible. It is often sub-classified as transactional and translation exposures.

- *Cash flow exposure*—This differs from accounting exposure because the items impacted are often still pending. For this reason, items subject to cash flow exposure cannot be easily valued. Currency mismatches involving revenues, expenses, bonuses, performance fees, and raw materials priced at market at time of delivery are examples of cash flow exposure. Whereas accounting exposure concerns historical events, cash flow exposure usually applies to future events, in other words, anticipated transactions that are not yet contracted.

- *Operating exposure*—This concerns the supply, demand, and price variables that affect sales performance, operational profitability, and competitive position. Identifying operating exposures involves questions such as: is the product still in the consumer's reach after a shift in foreign exchange? Is it easily substituted? Is it competitive? Are the competitors' prices denominated in the same currency? Are the competitors' costs denominated in the same currency?

- *Strategic exposure*—This relates more to perception than to a specific exposure. It concerns operating and cash flow exposures, but looks beyond the immediacy of accounting exposure. Unlike the more specific exposure concepts, the time horizon is measured in years. It involves not only current exchange rates, but expected exchange rates, trends in buying, trends in inflation, current competition, and potential competition. Strategic exposure focuses on the company's competitive position and comparative advantages, both now and in the future.

Foreign Currency Management

The concept of foreign currency management is quite straight forward. The first step is to identify the areas of operation subject to foreign exchange exposure. After discovering and analyzing the exposures, the decision is made as to what, if anything, to do about it. Some exposures might offset others, thereby reducing or eliminating the overall risk to the financial statements. Certain exposures, such as operating exposure, may endure for years, which may limit the available range of management tools. Other exposures might be better left unmanaged because managing them would create a more unacceptable exposure somewhere else.

Exposure, in a general sense, means that some segment of business is sensitive to currency exchange-rate fluctuation. The risk depends upon the potential degree of fluctuation. Risk, therefore, increases proportionately with an increase in the volatility of foreign exchange rates. Market turmoil may affect a currency directly, when resulting from a change in the fundamentals of that particular currency, or indirectly, such as when a currency gets caught up in a general market panic. In recent years, volatility in all major currencies has increased dramatically. Its effect on the U.S. dollar can be seen in Figure 1-1. Why has volatility increased in recent years? Some of the major causes are:

Figure 1-1: U.S. Dollar Index—Monthly
2/27/87 to 12/11/97*

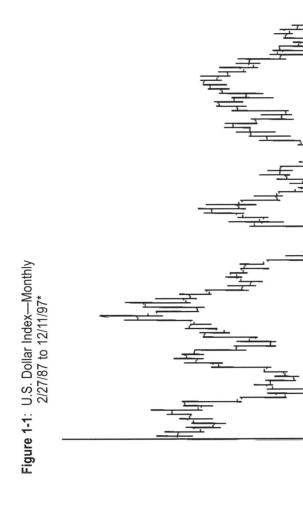

*Trade Weighted U.S. Dollar Index shows high degree of volatility from 1987 to 1997.

- Values of currencies of our major trading partners and of the U.S dollar are now governed by a floating rate regime. After the 1993 meltdown of the European Rate Mechanism (the official pricing matrix of various European currencies), virtually none of the major currencies remained officially fixed (or "pegged") in any meaningful way. Their rates of exchange are determined by ever-changing market forces which are political, economic, and psychological in nature.

- A massive volume of currency now exchanges hands on any given day. Currencies trade in the wake of efficient and instantaneous information flow. This flow does not readily differentiate among fact, rumor, and deception. Minor news items, even rumors, may quickly translate into major market moves before analysis can dampen the effect. The heavy volume, or *liquidity*, of the market may make exchange rate movements less violent than those of thinly traded markets, but it does not make a move any more predictable. Actually, greater liquidity may provide greater momentum once a trend gets under way, whether or not it is economically justified.

- Inherent in the growing volume of trading is the ability to almost instantly and effortlessly substitute one currency for another. Currencies flow rapidly and unimpeded in a single global market place. There is evidence that increasing the degree of substitutability in the international money supply may actually increase volatility beyond that which would otherwise occur because of the "band wagon" effect, where traders "pile on" to an emerging trend, increasing the volatility of the individual currencies involved.

This is today's world of foreign exchange. Its unpredictability creates risk for companies in every nation. Unpredictable rates of exchange can have an adverse effect on business or return on investment. This use to be the cost of "going offshore," but the distinction between global and domestic economies is fast disappearing. Today, a sudden change in the money markets of Bangkok or Seoul can disrupt the economic well-being of everyone from retail shop owners to mutual fund investors throughout the world, whether or not they ever venture out of town.

Prudent management dictates that business risk should be managed to whatever extent possible. "Managing risk" means finding a way to eliminate it or reduce it to acceptable levels. Foreign currency management techniques depend on how pervasive the risk is. It may be a one-time occurrence, for example, in an account payable or receivable, or it can be endemic to the operating structure of the organization.

Three Roads to a Hedge

Regardless of whether you deal with commercial accounts or restrict your business to personal investment and speculation, you probably understand the principles of risk management or "hedging." These principles lie at the core of currency management; however, the term "currency management" implies a somewhat broader concept which includes several methods of hedging, each appropriate for a particular type of exposure. One we call *transactional hedging*. This is your arena. Transactional hedging refers to exposure management through the purchase or sale of contracts, agreements, or financial instruments such as futures, options, forwards, and swaps. Transaction hedging is an effective management tool for accounting and, to a limited degree, cash flow exposures.

A second method involves the use of *operating strategies*. When the Japanese auto companies decided to protect their market by manufacturing in the United States, thereby eliminating the currency mismatch between costs and sales, they developed an operating strategy to hedge their exposure. The lead time required to implement such a strategy is measured in years. Operating strategies, therefore, are reserved for managing very long-term foreign exchange exposures in raw materials, production, and sales: in other words, strategic and operating exposures.

The third way currency exposure is hedged involves *financial adjustments*. In terms of time, planning, and commitment, this method is positioned midway between the first two. It is not as immediate or as flexible as transactional hedging, nor does it commit the company to a major undertaking such as those entailed in operating strategies. Changing U.S. dollar-denominated price sheets to Canadian dollar pricing, for example, is considered a financial adjustment. Adjusting accounting procedures so there is a lag in the collection of strong-currency receivables and an immediate collection of weak-currency receivables constitutes a financial adjustment. Cash flow and operating exposures are often best managed with some form of financial adjustment.

Transactional Hedging: An Example of How to Manage Accounting Exposure

A U.S. manufacturer of kitchenware signs a purchase order for plastic extrusion machinery to be purchased from a company in Hamburg, Germany. The cost of this machinery is 1,000,000 Deutsche marks. At this time, the rate of exchange is 0.50, or two Deutsche marks to the dollar. The price to the U.S. manufacturer, therefore, is $500,000.

The machines will be shipped in 6 months, with payment due upon arrival. For these six months—from the time of contract to the time of payment—the manufacturer has an exposure in Deutsche marks. If the rate stays the same, he will pay $500,000 as anticipated. If the Deutsche mark falls in value to $0.45 by the time the payment comes due, the manufacturer benefits. He will pay the DM1,000,000 as contracted, but the cost will be only $450,000, so he'll have a cost savings of $50,000. The risk, of course, is that the Deutsche mark might increase in value instead. If it is worth $0.55 when payment is due, the DM1,000,000 would now cost the manufacturer $550,000, causing a loss of $50,000.

This exposure may be handled in any number of ways.

1. The company may decide to remain exposed, affording the opportunity to gain if the Deutsche mark decreases in value.

2. The company may demand a clause be written into the sales agreement which indemnifies it for foreign exchange loss.

3. The company may decide to watch the market and take action only if the Deutsche mark begins an upward trend in value, or

4. It may hedge the transaction at the time the order is placed. A simple way to do this would be to exchange $500,000 for DM1,000,000 when the contract is signed, perhaps through the foreign exchange desk at the manufacturer's bank. The Deutsche marks are then deposited into a bank account established in Germany for that purpose, and paid out when the shipment is received. The exposure is eliminated, and the transaction is insulated from any potential changes in exchange rates, up or down. There is no unanticipated gain or loss.

Another way to achieve the same result is to buy the DM1,000,000 on credit. Let's say the manufacturer buys a *forward contract* from a commercial bank. He calls the bank and purchases the contract as soon as he finalizes his purchase contract for the extrusion equipment. The terms specify that the DM1,000,000 will be deposited into the manufacturer's German bank account six months later, the same as above. The Deutsche marks are not paid for until they are delivered. There is no real difference in payment terms between the purchase of the extrusion machinery and the purchase of the currency: the bank, like the German seller, extends credit to the manufacturer. Both machinery and currency are priced at the time of purchase and paid for upon delivery.

Six months later, when the payment for the machinery becomes due, the manufacturer sells the forward contract. In regard to the currency contract, he has a choice. He can pay for the Deutsche marks at the agreed-upon price of two to the dollar, and accept delivery of the currency. Upon his instructions, the Deutsche marks are deposited in the account of the German supplier to constitute payment. Alternatively, he can sell the currency back to the bank, and go out on his own to acquire the Deutsche marks, perhaps from a different source, to make the payment.

Let's say he chooses the latter course and sells the forward contract for the currency back to the bank. At the same time, he acquires DM1,000,000 and makes the payment for the equipment. If the Deutsche marks have increased in value and are now worth $0.55, his cost is $550,000 instead of the anticipated $500,000, but the price of the DM1,000,000 contract has also increased in value by roughly the same amount, which he sells it for a gain of $50,000. Consequently, there is no net loss.

By the same token, if the Deutsche marks fall to $0.45, the manufacturer pays out only $450,000; however, he sells the contract for $50,000 less than what he paid for it, and the bank debits his credit line for the difference. Thus, there is no net gain, either. The foreign currency exposure has been effectively hedged, and the payment is for the anticipated amount, no more, no less, whether measured in Deutsche marks or in dollars.

This example is called a "perfect hedge," which is something that is rarely attainable. The gain or loss from a hedge transaction seldom exactly offsets the gain or loss of the exchange rate move. The contract and the currency may change values at slightly different rates. Also, there are possible tax implications involving the market transaction, and there are always transaction costs to consider. Regardless, if the hedge is properly constructed, these factors are insignificant compared to the reduction in risk exposure.

Figure 1-2

Exposure to a Deutsche mark Liability

Purchase Machinery for DM 1000,000
with Payment due in 6 Months
Current Exchange Rate: 1 US $ = 2 DM

Mfg	bank	Supplier
Debit $ Acct to Buy Deutsche marks	Exchange $US for DM	Credit DM Acct DM 1,000,000

Bank transactions six months later.
Question: How many U.S.$ to be debited from mfg acct?

Figure 1-3

Solution # 1

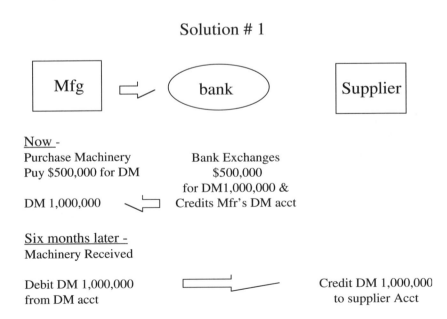

Now -
Purchase Machinery
Puy $500,000 for DM

DM 1,000,000

Bank Exchanges
$500,000
for DM1,000,000 &
Credits Mfr's DM acct

Six months later -
Machinery Received

Debit DM 1,000,000
from DM acct

Credit DM 1,000,000
to supplier Acct

Figure 1-4

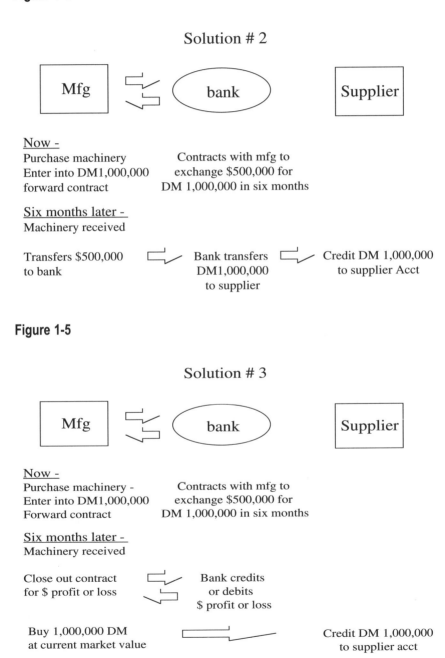

Solution # 2

Mfg   bank   Supplier

Now -
Purchase machinery   Contracts with mfg to
Enter into DM1,000,000   exchange $500,000 for
forward contract   DM 1,000,000 in six months

Six months later -
Machinery received

Transfers $500,000   Bank transfers   Credit DM 1,000,000
to bank   DM1,000,000   to supplier Acct
                            to supplier

Figure 1-5

Solution # 3

Mfg   bank   Supplier

Now -
Purchase machinery -   Contracts with mfg to
Enter into DM1,000,000   exchange $500,000 for
Forward contract   DM 1,000,000 in six months

Six months later -
Machinery received

Close out contract   Bank credits
for $ profit or loss   or debits
                            $ profit or loss

Buy 1,000,000 DM   Credit DM 1,000,000
at current market value   to supplier acct

Is Hedging the Answer?

The above example illustrates a problem of much greater magnitude than the imprecision of offsetting gains and losses. This problem underlies all risk management programs. Simply put, should the hedge be entered in the first place? Does it benefit the manufacturer? Only hindsight reveals the answer. If the dollar made a major advance against the Deutsche mark while the hedge was in place, it would produce a loss of major proportions. The fact that it was offset by a savings somewhere else may not be enough justification, especially when the loss, or "hedge burden" as it is sometimes known, is being explained to a senior manager who has had no input in the risk management program. This is the single biggest obstacle to foreign currency management. Unless there are clearly defined objectives, safeguards in place, and clear communications among the various levels of management, a hedging program can end up as a non-starter at best and a financial disaster at worst.

The record is littered with casualties. In 1984, Lufthansa had placed a major purchase order for airliners from a U.S. firm. Its economists were forecasting a stronger dollar. Perhaps aware of Laker Air's experience, it locked up the Deutschemark/dollar exchange rate with a forward contract. The economists guessed wrong. In one year, Lufthansa had lost somewhere around $150 million, and one or two financial managers reportedly lost their jobs. Separately, the chairman of Porsche found himself unemployed two years later. He had engineered the company into a dependence on the U.S. market for 61% of its revenue without hedging against a downturn in the dollar. Porsche suffered a major financial setback as a result. It was about that same time that Volkswagon began sorting through a loss of $259 million which lined the pockets of a group of currency traders who had falsified documents in an illegal "bucket shop" operation. Meanwhile, in the United States, Zenith Electronics Corporation was explaining to its stockholders a $13 million loss on a forward contract. Jerry K. Pearlman, chairman and president, remarked that "it's the kind of mistake we will never make again."[4] It's a "damned if you do and damned if you don't" situation, and it's no wonder that U.S. corporate officers would just rather forget the whole thing.

Conclusion

It is evident that ignoring currency rates while engaging in international business is no longer a viable option. Simply staying out of foreign markets is no guarantee against foreign exchange risk, as discovered by

Chrysler Corporation. Invoicing international sales solely in U.S dollars might well bring about an exposure even more risky than that incurred from transacting in foreign currencies. As the manager who spoke at the export seminar discovered, that solution simply turns very visible accounting exposure into less visible, harder-to-manage operating exposure. No matter how exposure is viewed, foreign currency management indisputably will play an increasingly essential role in today's new business environment. In spite of the pitfalls and the war stories, the number of companies today who successfully hedge their exposures, large or small, is continuing to mushroom.

Exposure to foreign currency risk is created by lack of predictability in the foreign exchange markets. Exchange rates have become much more volatile and unpredictable as a result of government policies, large and continuous capital flows, and instantaneous convertibility. Moreover, a single business entity can experience different exposures, each affecting a different aspect of the business. Results from these exposures can range from windfall to insolvency. The outcome is never certain. Management techniques to reduce or eliminate exposure will differ, according to the perspective of the company. Although short-term transactions can be hedged with market transactions, longer-term risks often require permanent changes in operation.

Most importantly, foreign currency management must mesh with the overall policy of the company. In many cases, there is no policy to refer to, and one must be developed. Hedging currencies is done properly by implementing a program that has been reviewed, accepted, and understood by all levels of management. Senior management must be involved, if not in the tactical decisions, certainly in the strategic ones. Everyone must understand the possible consequences of every "what if" scenario. Controls must be implemented and authority to make decisions in a timely fashion must be granted. Perhaps the most difficult part of implementing a foreign currency management program is presentation of the concept. For this reason, it often takes a year or more from presentation to implementation of a program.

Achieving these objectives means that you, as the hedge advisor, must first assume the role of financial consultant for the prospective corporate client. It is by your efforts that the financial manager will understand—and be able to explain to peers and superiors—the concepts, the objectives, and the possible results of a foreign currency management program.

CHAPTER 2

The Competitive Edge

There are numerous prospects out there. What they have in common is a financial risk of loss due to foreign currency exposures. This prospective market consists of businesses that engage in international contracting, financing, investment, sales, and purchasing. When we add in those with competitive exposure, it includes many of the "all domestic" companies as well. These prospects range in size from large multinationals to the proprietorship down the street. The segment that may be the fastest growing is the mid-sized corporation. For the first time, companies in this size category are seriously embarking on ventures in the overseas market place. Mid-sized is defined as firms with annual sales between $15 million and $100 million. They span a variety of industries, including manufacturing, financial services, retail, and agriculture.

Not only is this segment of the market the fastest growing, it is the most accessible in your development of new business. The management layers common to a large multinational are not yet firmly set (the treasurer still answers his own phone). This market is substantial. You can prove it to yourself by picking up the latest copy of the local manufacturer's directory. Count the number of companies reporting annual sales above $100 million. Then count the number with sales between $15 million and $100 million. The latter will outnumber the former many times over. This is significant because prospecting is still a numbers game.

There are two additional reasons for considering mid-sized corporations as your primary market. First, the trend in foreign currency management is trickling down from multinationals to mid-sized companies. The need is growing, but most of the time these smaller firms have neither the in-house expertise nor the large banking relationships required to develop a well-thought-out risk management program. As newcomers, they may not even know who to call for advice. The door is wide open to the financial service provider who can ask the right questions and give the right answers.

Secondly, your major competitor for this business is the nearest commercial bank or brokerage office that has a foreign exchange capability. Fortunately, you will find they are pursuing only the larger multinational corporations. The competition for these accounts can be formidable. This is not the case with mid-sized corporations. They are waiting for someone to come through the door. They are not that finicky. If you can only speak knowledgeably about this business, you have a clear competitive edge. Not many in the financial service industry can do so. This book provides you with that edge.

The Currency Markets

The banking, securities, insurance, and other financial industries are all involved in the four major currency markets. These four markets are interconnected and share price discovery. Foreign exchange takes place both within and among the markets. They are distinguished primarily by their participants, operating procedures, and locations. The purpose of these markets is identical: to exchange one currency for another at an agreed upon rate (price).

One market is the *cash market*. It operates in a straight-forward fashion. Seeing how foreign exchange occurs in this market place helps in understanding the others. The cash market usually is found in the international departments of a bank's branch offices. More recently, automatic teller machines also do the job. Here, two currencies simply, literally, change hands. The foreign exchange booths astride the Canadian-U.S. boarder are examples of cash market operations. Standing at the counter, travelers from one country buy a nominal amount of the other country's currency to make cash purchases of goods.

The rate of exchange at which the currency changes hands is determined by what goes on in another, much larger, currency market: the *interbank*. Sometimes referred to as *Forex*, the interbank operates much like the cash market, and with the same purpose, except that there is no physical exchange of currency, but only of *currency deposits*. The currency itself rarely leaves the country of origin. Instead, participants set up various bank accounts in different countries, then transfer deposits from one account to another by exchanging the appropriate currencies. These exchanges involve wire transfers which normally take a couple of days to complete. For this reason, cash transactions are known as *spot* transactions, with "spot" referring to an exchange that settles in two business days (or, in the case of U.S.—Canadian dollar transactions, in one business day).

A forward contract hedge is an interbank transaction identical in every respect to a spot transaction except it settles *more* than two business days in the future. The transfer can take place from three business days to five years or more in the future.

There is also the *over-the-counter* market. Here is where non-standard currency agreements are traded. The word "traded" may be a misnomer. "Assigned" may be a better term because the secondary market for customized contracts is thin to non-existent. The over-the-counter market can be best described as a meeting ground where two business entities come together and contract with each other. It is the workshop in which complex currency options, swaps, and other derivatives are engineered, packaged, and sold to commercial interests world wide. These instruments are in written agreement form, not traded orally by phone. Some of the plainer types have become quasi-standardized through such market-making intermediary organizations as the International Swap Dealers Association (ISDA). Regardless of the product, they all share one common characteristic: their values are derived from the day-to-day price discovery of the interbank spot transaction.

The last and, for you who are brokers, the most important market consists of the futures and options exchanges. The Chicago Mercantile Exchange (CME) is the major exchange-traded currency market in the United States. An up-and-coming player, especially in emerging market currencies, is the FINEX, financial division of the New York Cotton Exchange (FINEX). The MidAmerica Commodity Exchange (MidAm) also has a place in foreign currency management, as does the cash option market of the Philadelphia Stock Exchange (PHLX). Cash currency options exercise into the spot market through the interbank the same way options on futures are exercised for the underlying futures contract. The concept of futures contracts continues to broaden. The CME introduced a "rolling spot" contract that replicates the interbank spot/next swap. More recently, the CME rolled out a currency forward contract that settles by conversion into the underlying rolling spot contract. The effect is virtually indistinguishable from the settlement of an interbank forward.

The Interbank

When considering the currency market segments, the interbank may be visualized as a cake, and the other markets as thin layers of frosting. In 1992, more than one trillion dollars worth of foreign currency transactions took place daily.[1] The interbank accounted for 96% of this total, the majority of which were exchanges in spot. Within the United States, 51% of all interbank transactions involved spot transactions, with an additional 32% identified as swap transactions. Of the remainder, 8% consisted of options on interbank transactions, and the balance were forward contracts (the "plain vanilla" corporate hedge vehicle). While this is only 5% of the market, which has a total daily notional volume equivalent to 960 billion dollars, there are almost $50 billion dollars worth of forward trades *every day*.

The interbank is sometimes referred to as "FOREX," although that acronym more accurately designates an association of interbank participants. Some simply refer to it as the "foreign exchange market." The interbank is comprised of a global network of commercial, investment, and merchant banks, along with a number of multinational corporations and other financial institutions. There is no central location, but simply a communication network. There are no floors, no currency pits, there is no open outcry. Currencies are exchanged by phone and computer. Because the interbank is a free-floating global market, it is unregulated by any government. Short of barring international currency trading, government regulators have no practical way to control it. (This does not mean they've stopped looking for one.)

Not all commercial banks are members of this network. It is primarily the domain of large international, national, and regional financial firms. Although its transactional services are sometimes extended to local branches to provide foreign exchange access to retail customers, the actual trading remains centralized at a dealing desk in the financial firm's main office.

Singapore, Hong Kong, Zurich, Frankfort, London, New York, and most major financial centers in between are on stream. The interbank never closes; the off hours are the non-business hours, the nights, and the holidays that roll slowly in and out of certain areas of the web. The trading volume is overwhelming. It easily absorbs transactions of such "customers" as the Federal Reserve Board and other central banks. After a few brief days of battle in August, 1993, France, its foreign reserves exhausted, went down in glorious defeat defending the *franc fort*. It was interbank trading that did it in. Four years later, a block of Asian nations, including Korea, Thailand, Malaysia, Indonesia, waged similar battles with similar conclusions.

All but about 4% of global foreign exchange takes place on the interbank network. The rest is divided among the futures, options, and stock exchanges around the world. Outright trading in forward contracts generates more transactions than all the futures and options exchanges in all countries, yet it comprises only 5% of the total interbank business. It is no wonder that currency futures traders keep a constant eye on this market.

The Foreign Exchange Broker

One participant in the interbank market is the foreign exchange broker. This person acts in the same capacity as any securities or futures broker. He is the intermediary between principals in a transaction. He brings the buyer and seller together, facilitating the transaction. For his efforts, he receives a commission paid by the principals. He doesn't realize a profit or loss on the transaction and has no economic interest in which way the market goes. Firms and individuals act as brokers on the interbank for a clientele of banks. Through their efforts, bank dealers find counterparts for transactions or acquire current information about the market.

The interbank system contains "resting orders," similar to those on an exchange. These are open orders as yet unfilled, awaiting a specific price. They are posted as bids (or "buys") and offers ("sells"). The broker's role is to keep track of the current bids and offers, which are continuously updated and displayed on a computer monitor in a "quote stream." In response to an inquiry as to where the market is, he will report the highest bid and lowest offer currently displayed. To maintain confidentiality, he does not divulge the names of the banks making the bids or offers until a trade actually occurs. In very lightly traded markets, the broker often performs the additional service of phoning various banks trying to find a buyer or seller to fill a client order. Brokers need volume to sustain their business, and normally restrict their efforts to the key currencies.

The Foreign Exchange Dealer

Most participating banks in the interbank market act as dealers. The term *dealer* refers to both the bank and to the individual trader. Most foreign exchange dealers are employed by banks or by other financial institutions such as large brokerage houses. Some work for smaller, private firms or are self-employed. The primary difference between a broker and a dealer is method of compensation. Whereas the broker receives commissions, a dealer receives a "cut" on the deal.Because the dealer is a principal or trades on behalf of a principal, he places his firm's money at risk. Dealers may deal directly with other dealers or banks, or through a broker. There are a number of ways an agreement may be reached. The dealer, who we'll assume works for a bank:

1. is a market maker and responds to an inquiry for a quote from another dealer;

2. is an in-house or proprietary trader and takes a position seeking to profit from price changes in the market;

3. generates transactions for revenue by capturing spreads between bids and offers while offsetting market risk in his portfolio through other dealers;

4. initiates a transaction to obtain currency required for his bank's international operations;

5. responds to a client order to buy or sell a currency;

6. initiates a transaction to cover or offset a previous transaction for a client or with another dealer or broker.

The Market Maker

The dealer network runs on reciprocity. A major bank dealer is expected to make a market in the currencies he trades. As a market maker, he gives two quotes in response to an inquiry from another dealer. These represent the price at which he'll buy (bid) and the (somewhat higher) price at which he'll sell (offer). It's easy to see the importance of reciprocity. If a dealer is less than forthright in naming both prices, he'll soon receive very few inquiries. Moreover, he will find it more difficult to obtain fair prices when he makes his own inquiries to other dealers. Some U.S. branches of foreign banks act as market makers for their home currencies. This is especially important for small countries with infrequently traded currencies. The market maker is entrusted to stand behind the currency as the dealer of last resort, always available to either buy or sell upon request.

Interbank Operations

Banks are notoriously unwilling risk takers. Although bank dealers may be very agile in the fast-paced world of foreign exchange, the risk of loss from a major move in exchange rates is quite often unacceptable. The quantities of currency traded in a single day by one individual can easily amount to hundreds of millions of dollars. In these amounts, an adverse move could substantially change the quarterly earnings of a fair-sized bank; therefore, rather than looking to profit from changes in exchange rates, most banks generate revenues from the *spread* between the offer and the bid. Buying currency for resale (or selling currency for repurchase) is conceptually no different from borrowing money at one price (interest rate) and lending it out at another. In the fast-paced world of foreign exchange, however, there is no assurance that currency can be resold or repurchased at a profit if it is held for more than a few seconds. Banks rarely buy and hold for very long. When they buy $1,000,000 worth of currency, they often resell it as quickly as possible. If the exchange constitutes a loan, both transactions are made simultaneously.

Let's assume that a U.S. bank—we'll call it *Downtown Bank*—discovers that it must deposit 3,000,000 Deutsche marks with its correspondent bank in Frankfort, Germany, for thirty days to satisfy a customer's instructions. Not having the currency, it must acquire it. Downtown calls *Crosstown Bank* and asks for a two-way spot quote on Deutsche marks. Since the currency is only required for 30 days, Downtown also asks for a quote on the 30-day forward rate.The following quote is given for spot: "67 bid, ask 71." The response to the query on 30-day forward pricing is, "plus 46." What do these cryptic numbers signify?

Interbank Quotes

If we turn to the futures page in the *Wall Street Journal* to find a currency price, we find the price quoted in dollar terms. In other words, if the Deutsche mark for the nearest month closed yesterday at 7108, we understand that one Deutsche mark is worth $0.7108. This is a *direct quote*. The interbank, however, gives the same quote *indirectly* in Deutsche mark terms. The indirect quote reflects the number of Deutsche marks that are equal in value to one U.S. dollar.

These two quotes are reciprocals of each other. Converting between direct and indirect quotes involves a simple calculator operation. You can change the futures price of .7108 to its indirect equivalent with the following steps on a calculator:

1. Enter "100."

2. Key in "divide."

3. Enter "7108" (ignore the decimal point for now).

4. Then "equals."

5. Move the decimal two places to the right.

The answer is 1.40687. Customarily, interbank quotes are rounded to the fourth decimal place, so the indirect quote for the Deutsche mark becomes 1.4069. We can go the other way as well. If you follow the same steps, substituting "14069" for "7108," the answer becomes "0.007108." Again, move the decimal two places to the right. If we forget where to place the decimal, we can deduce where it belongs by knowing approximately how many units of one currency are equivalent to one unit of the other.

The interbank dealer does not transact at spot, of course, but at a spread, marking down his buy price (bid) and marking up his sell price (offer) from spot, which is the mid-price. In keeping with the fast pace of the markets, dealers work in short hand, much like floor traders. They assume the person inquiring knows about where the market is. So, rather than quoting the entire number, dealers respond with only the part that varies from moment to moment, which is the last two or three digits. Therefore, "67 bid ask 71" translates as "I will buy at 1.4067 and sell at 1.4071." From a spot price of 7108, then, we obtain the following quotes:

Bid 1.4067   Spot 1.4069   Offer 1.4071

Just as currency futures prices vary with different delivery months, the 30-day forward price is rarely the same as the spot price. In our example, the dealer quote for 30-day forward is "46 pips" (or "ticks"). Note that the dealer gives the spread only once, and it is based on spot. The forward points are given as a constant. They are added to (or subtracted from) whichever price is pertinent to the quote—the spot, the bid, or the offer; therefore, the 30-day forward mid-price (spot) is 1.4069 plus 46 points (1.4115), the 30-day bid is 1.4067 plus 46 points (1.4113), and the 30-day offer is 1.4071 plus 46 (1.4117). We can now compare interbank prices with futures prices as follows:

Spot Quote: "67 bid, ask 71"

	Spot	*Bid*	*Offer*
indirect	1.4069	1.40**67**	1.40**71**
direct	.71078	.71088	.71068

30-day Forward Quote: "Plus 46"

	Spot+ 46	*Bid+* 46	*Offer+* 46
indirect	1.4115	1.4**113**	1.4**117**
direct	.70847	.70857	.70837

Based on the direct quote, the dealer's bid appears to be higher than the offer; however, the dealer does not bid or offer Deutsche marks, but U.S. dollars. A "67 bid" essentially means that "I will buy 1,000,000 dollars for 1,406,700 Deutsche marks." This custom of bidding and offering dollars means the bid is lower than the offer.

Knowing the difference in pricing techniques between the interbank and the exchanges is crucial to anyone who deals in both markets. A currency hedger who is used to futures prices can easily misinterpret the dealer's quote when he hears, "67 bid ask 71." Usually, however, corporate clients are not given both prices. Dealers know their quotes are often shopped around. By restricting quotes to single bids or offers, the dealer's profit is not disclosed to competitors nor to customers, who are often unaware of the precise spot value at the time of the quote.

Dealers speak to each other in code, but the language tends to be more precise when they deal with clients. The bank dealer will ask the client whether he is buying or selling, and then give the price at which the bank will deal by such statements such as "I will sell you 30-day Deutsche marks at 1.4113." Trouble arises when the dealer quotes forward prices to an unsophisticated customer without taking the time to communicate clearly. A client once insisted that a competing bank was offering to sell him British pounds 6 months out at a rate substantially below the market. Spot was approximately at 1.37, and he was quoted 1.35. He asked the bank to confirm the quote, and it came back the same. Finally, after questioning, it became apparent that the dealer was quoting the six-month forward *points*, 135 over spot, which the client had had mistaken for the actual exchange rate.

The spreads in dealer-to-dealer spot quotes for large currency amounts can be very narrow. They are wider for forward transactions. This reflects the additional market risk of carrying future positions or, in this case, forward positions. Quotes for forwards of one year or longer may carry very wide spreads to account for the high risk and low trading volume of distant value dates. It is not uncommon for spreads to be two hundred points or more, depending on volume. Because of these exceedingly wide spreads, most activity centers around spot and forwards up to 90 days.

Exchange Rates and Cross Rates

During an exchange of currencies, it is the exchange rate that is being quoted, either directly or indirectly. In all markets, the term "exchange rate" is understood to mean the conversion value of two currencies, one of which is the U.S. dollar. A "cross rate," on the other hand, is a rate of exchange between two currencies, neither of which is the U.S. dollar. Cross rates are discovered by factoring the dollar out of the equation. The table below is an example of what you might see in the Wall Street Journal. You can find each of the cross rates listed by multiplying the indirect quote of one currency by the direct quote of the other. For example, multiply the indirect quote of the Swiss franc (1.1628) by the direct quote of the British pound (1.5995) and you obtain 1.8599. This is the SF/£ cross rate, or the number of Swiss francs per British pound.

By convention, foreign exchange dealers around the world quote a currency price as a function of the U.S. dollar. In other words, they quote the exchange rate. If asked for a cross rate bid, they first find the exchange rates of the two currencies and, through them, the cross rate.

Key Currency Cross Rates Late New York Trading June 15, 1995

	Dollar	Pound	SFranc	Guilder	Peso	Yen	Lira	D-Mark	FFranc	CdnDlr
Canada	1.3778	2.2038	1.18490	.87535	.22313	.01631	.00084	.98064	.27959	...
France	4.9280	7.882	4.2380	3.1309	.79806	.05833	.00299	3.5075	...	3.5767
Germany	1.4050	2.2473	1.2083	.89263	.22753	.01663	.00085	...	.28511	1.0197
Italy	1649.5	2638.4	1418.56	1047.97	267.13	19.525	...	1174.02	334.72	1197.2
Japan	84.48	135.13	72.652	53.672	13.681	...	.05122	60.128	17.143	61.32
Mexico	6.1750	9.8769	5.3105	3.9231	...	.07309	.00374	4.3950	1.2530	4.4818
Netherlands	1.5740	2.5176	1.3536	...	.25490	.01863	.00095	1.1203	.31940	1.1424
Switzerland	1.1628	1.8599	...	.73875	.18831	.01376	.00070	.82762	.23596	.8440
U.K.	.62520	...	.53766	.39720	.10125	.00740	.00038	.44498	.12687	.45376
U.S.	...	1.5995	.85999	.63532	.16194	.01184	.00061	.71174	.20292	.72579

Source: Dow Jones Telerate Inc., from *Wall Street Journal* June 15, 1995

The rates listed in the vertical columns are quoted indirectly. For example, there are 1.3778 Canadian dollars in one U.S. dollar. The rates listed horizontally are directly quoted. (The value of one Canadian dollar is $0.72579). You can demonstrate that these two numbers are reciprocals: multiplying the direct quote by the indirect quote will always produce 1.00.

The Foreign Exchange Swap

Returning to the Crosstown Bank quotes on page 34, the Downtown Bank finds that the quotes are in line, and makes the deal. Remember, Downtown needs to acquire the foreign currency and therefore sells dollars for Deutsche marks at Crosstown's dollar bid of 1.4067. It only needs the currency for 30 days, so it simultaneously enters into a second transaction to buy back dollars (and sell Deutsche marks) at Crosstown's 30-day forward offer of 1.4117.

The two banks have completed a two-way transaction which futures brokers know as a calendar spread trade. In the interbank, it is referred to as a *swap*, or, more specifically, a *foreign exchange swap*. Not unexpectedly, this type of transaction is far more common between banks than taking outright forward positions. Banks are established to borrow and lend money, which is precisely what the swap accomplishes.

Two days after the deal takes place, the accounts are settled. Crosstown transfers 3,000,000 Deutsche marks from its German-based account to the Frankfort account specified in Downtown's delivery instructions. In turn, Downtown debits $2,132,640(equal to 3,000,000 times the exchange rate of.71088) from its domestic foreign exchange account and credits the funds to Crosstown's domestic foreign exchange account.

Thirty days later, both banks reverse the original trade. Downtown transfers 3,000,000 Deutsche marks to Crosstown's Frankfort account, and Crosstown credits$2,125,110 (3,000,000 times the rate of .70837) to Downtown's domestic account. Crosstown realizes a dollar gain of $7,530 on the swap, reflecting a $1,930 profit plus $5,600 to compensate for 30 days lost interest on the Deutsche marks.

You may recognize this operation for what it really is: a currency hedge by both banks. Assuming that both Downtown and Crosstown start out with balanced Deutsche mark accounts, the spot trade, by itself, creates a foreign exchange exposure for both. Downtown contracts a Deutsche mark asset, and Crosstown acquires a Deutsche mark liability, since it has to debit its account to deliver the currency. The forward leg of the spread simply hedges the spot trade by locking in the return price; therefore, no subsequent change in exchange rates will affect the account balance. As with any spread position, the exchange gains or losses in one leg are offset by the opposing losses and gains in the other, as long as both prices rise and fall together.

There are several different types of foreign exchange swaps, each tailored to the needs of the participating banks. A *spot/next* swap exchanges currency in two business days, and reverses the trade the third day. A *tomorrow/next* swap exchanges currency the next business day and reverses the trade the following day. (Remember: only U.S./Canadian dollar transactions take place the following day. All other spot transactions require two business days.) A bank or its client who expects to meet a foreign currency liability within the next two weeks or so, but is uncertain of the exact date, may transact a series of tomorrow/next swaps day after day until the payment is made. Each day, the swap offsets the swap from the previous day. This procedure is known as a *roll over.* Other swaps are *spot/forward,* as in our example above, or *forward/forward,* in which a forward contract is initiated and reversed at a more distant forward date.

Rolling Over a Tomorrow / Next Swap

Trade Date		Buy	Sell	Value Date
1-Feb	Canadian dollar		2,000,000	2-Feb
	Canadian dollar	2,000,000		3-Feb
2-Feb	Canadian dollar		2,000,000	3-Feb
	Canadian dollar	2,000,000		4-Feb
3-Feb	Canadian dollar		2,000,000	4-Feb
	Canadian dollar	2,000,000		5-Feb
4-Feb	Canadian dollar		2,000,000	5-Feb
	Canadian dollar	2,000,000		8-Feb

Dates shown reflect the "good value" dates beginning with Monday, February 2nd.

Downtown Bank enters a swap in which it sells Canadian dollars value dated the next business day, and buys them back the following business day. It can roll the trade forward an unlimited number of times by repeatedly selling and then buying in through tomorrow/next swaps. No currency changes hands until the last swap of the series has settled. The exchange rates used to price each swap always differ by one day. Downtown pays the bid and buys the offer, thereby incurring a transaction cost each time.

Interbank vs. Exchange Contracts

The bank enjoys one competitive advantage over futures brokers in servicing corporate hedgers: the selection of available currencies. The dealers in the interbank are able to make a market in virtually every freely-traded currency. By contrast, the U.S. futures exchanges have a limited selection. In 1997, just eleven currencies were listed on the Chicago Mercantile Exchange. The U.S. Dollar Index and a handful of other currency contracts are found on the Philadelphia Stock Exchange and the FINEX. Perhaps another forty trade on exchanges overseas, with much duplication between them. Furthermore, many exchange-traded currency contracts are inactive or illiquid. Still, when a prospective corporate hedger is exposed to one of the more liquid exchange-traded currencies, the playing field quickly levels.

Category	Interbank	Exchange
1 - Currencies	All freely-traded currencies	Limited selection, not all active or liquid
2 - Spot transactions	Available	Limited - liquidity varies*
3 - Forward transactions	Forward contracts	Futures contracts
4 - Spread transactions: spot and forward / forward	Spot /forward swaps / Forward /forward swaps	Limited - liquidity varies* / Calendar spreads
5 - Cross rate transactions	Available	Crossrate futures contracts and inter-market spreads
6 - Options	Customized options for all transactions	Customized / standardized options both spot & futures

*The CME has introduced rolling spot contracts and options, as well as currency forward contracts. Rolling spot replicates the interbank spot/next swap which automatically rolls over unless offset or delivered upon. The currency forward contract specifies delivery of a rolling spot contract. Both of these contracts trade like futures, but are quoted indirectly. Rolling spot contracts are accounted for as spot/next swaps; in addition to the normal market value fluctuation, the one-day forward point spread is credited or debited daily. At this time, these contracts trade actively only in Deutsche marks.

While the banking industry's primary interest is fixing the exchange rate for lending and borrowing purposes through swaps, the corporate hedger is more interested in forward pricing. A hedge locks in one side of the transaction in the market, not both. The other side, of course, is the business exposure; therefore, the hedger transacts in outright forward contracts and options the vast majority of the time. It is in the area of forward pricing that the exchange is best equipped to compete through futures contracts, futures options, and cash options.

Even for exchange-traded currencies, the interbank enjoys some competitive advantages in a direct comparison of product features. There are a number of other areas, however, in which the exchange has the edge. Let's compare the competitive advantages of the basic exchange and interbank products—forward contracts and futures contracts.

Forward Contracts vs. Futures Contracts

The market with the competitive advantage for mid-sized corporate clients:

Contract Specifications	Futures Exchange
Settlement Date	Interbank
Early Liquidation	Futures Exchange
Distribution	Futures Exchange
Settlement Procedures	Interbank
Transaction Costs	Futures Exchange
Credit Risk	Futures Exchange
Regulatory Oversight	Futures Exchange

Let's look at the comparative features for each of these categories. The contract with the greater competitive advantage is underlined.

Contract Specifications

Forwards

Quasi-standardized contracts can be denominated either in a fixed dollar amount or in foreign currency units. There is no standardized amount, but dealers customarily trade in increments of $1,000,000. Anything smaller cannot be easily laid off, and thus involves a market risk to the dealer. For this reason, dealers may not accept business under $1,000,000 in value, or they may compensate for the greater risk by quoting wider spreads.

Futures

Standard contract size denominated in foreign currency units. Transactions can be for any number of contracts. Incremental sizes are quite suitable as hedging vehicles for most mid-sized corporations, although some over-hedging or under-hedging may be necessary. Alternatively, MidAm contracts and PHLX options are available at half the standard size of CME contracts; FINEX contracts for certain currencies are larger. Compare the $1,000,000 interbank minimum with the following CME futures contract values:

Currency*	No. of Units	Close	$ value
Australian dollar	100,000	.6749	$67,490
British pound	62,500	1.6842	$105,262
Canadian dollar	100,000	.7033	$70,330
Deutsche mark	125,000	.5628	$70,350
Japanese yen	12,500,000	.007768	$97,100
Mexican peso	500,000	.12185	$60,925
Swiss franc	125,000	.6991	$87,387
U.S. dollar index (FINEX)	1000 x index	89.73	$98,410

*Nearest contract as of December 1st, 1997.

Settlement Date

Forwards

Contracts are settled on the "value date," which can be any "good date" from three days to seven years in the future. A good date is one on which the banks are open for business in both countries. Note that certain "even-dated" forwards are listed by most price quote services. These carry the value dates of 30 days (from spot), 60 days, 90 days, 180 days, etc. They serve two purposes: (1) The even dates give a "snap shot" representation of the forward price, in the same manner futures contracts do; (2) They provide a standardized dated instrument for trading purposes; however, once traded, an even dated forward—like every other forward—is identified by the specific value date for settlement purposes. For example, a 30-day forward, contracted on June 7, 1995 now becomes a July 07, 1995 forward. On July 7th it converts to spot and is offset, rolled over, or delivered.

Futures

Only four settlement dates (last trading dates) are available for actively traded contracts. These are the third Monday of the fiscal quarter months of March, June, September, and December.

Early Liquidation

Forwards

Contracts can be offset at anytime, the same as futures contracts. A transaction that initiates an opposite position in the same amount *for the same specific value date* effectively offsets both contracts; however, offset does not mean settled. Both contracts must remain open until their value date. No disbursement of funds takes place until that time; therefore, any unrealized gains or losses remain unrealized until the value date. This delayed settlement procedure can tie up a customer's credit line until the value date becomes spot.

Futures

Contracts can be liquidated by offset at anytime, with settlement occurring at the time of offset.

Distribution of Gains and Losses

Forwards

A credit line is established with the bank for transaction purposes. Transactions are marked to the market daily, with resulting credits and debits posted to the line of credit. Funds are required if market losses exceed the credit limits; however, unrealized gains are not distributed until the value date, whether or not the positions have been previously offset.

Futures

A margin account is established with the broker. Transactions are marked to the market daily, with resulting credits and debits entered in the account. A minimum margin value must be maintained in the account. Initial margin requirements can be satisfied with treasury bills deposited in a collateral account. (Maintenance margins must be satisfied in cash, as with all futures contracts.) The broker's competitive advantage is the distribution of unrealized gains, which are payable to the client upon demand as long as margin requirements are satisfied.

Settlement Procedures

Forwards

Settlement on the value date can be by previous offset or by delivery. Transactions in the United States are dollar denominated. Delivery is the routine procedure. If delivery is elected, the contracted amount of foreign currency is transferred by wire to an account within the currency's home country as specified by the buyer. If the client is selling dollars and buying foreign currency, the bank debits a dollar amount from the client's credit line, with the amount based upon the exchange rate in effect at the time of trade. If the client buys dollars and sells foreign currency, the bank credits dollars in the same fashion. Of course, the balance also reflects the credits and debits that have accrued from daily marking the position to the market until the date of settlement. Although delivery is the routine method of settlement, the positions can be offset at any time.

Futures

Settlement results immediately from offset or by delivery after the last trading date. Procedures for making delivery are identical to those with forwards, with the broker crediting or debiting the margin account. Offset is routine. (Although delivery is possible, it is usually discouraged by the broker.) The efficient delivery procedures of the interbank allow the client to close out exposed receivables and payables more expeditiously, giving the competitive advantage to the bank. It is important, therefore, that a broker knows how his firm handles delivery requests for futures contracts and smooth the way, should a client elect to take that option.

Transaction Costs

Forwards

Dealers often bid competitively for transactions of $1,000,000 or more. Two and a half "pips" are the usual spread, equivalent to approximately a half a point on a futures contract. (If $1,000,000 is equivalent to, say, 1,500,000 foreign currency units, a half point equals $75).In lesser dollar amounts, transaction costs can climb substantially, putting the hedge under water before the rate even changes. The cost is not disclosed, but becomes part of the quote.

Futures

Flat fee commissions based on number of contracts are the rule. The commission is always disclosed to the client, and is taken from a fixed schedule—a big selling point for the broker. *A major advantage* is the low cost for contracts of relatively small amounts of currency.

Risk of Contract Default

Forwards

The credit worthiness of the dealer should be a consideration. The transaction is between two private parties: the corporation and the bank. There is no third party to guarantee performance. Either of the parties can default, producing a loss to the other.

Futures

Credit risk to the client is virtually non-existent because of the clearinghouse. The clearinghouse for the exchange is backed both jointly and individually by every futures clearing member of that exchange. In the case of the CME, that is practically the entire futures brokerage industry. Again, in an era when insolvency due to derivative trading is commonplace, this is an important competitive advantage.

Regulatory Oversight

Forwards

The interbank extends beyond international borders and will almost certainly remain unregulated by any sovereignty. Governmental attempts to regulate the market will probably just drive trading offshore. No license or examination is required to deal in interbank foreign exchange.

Futures

The exchanges are heavily government regulated. Regardless of how confining that may be, a corporate client may find this regulatory oversight reassuring.

Different Markets, Different Values
Futures Prices (Currency)
Thursday, June 15, 1995

	Open	High	Low	Settle	Change	Lifetime High	Low	Open Interest
British Pound (CME) - 62,500 pds.; $ per pound								
June	1.6074	1.6074	1.5920	1.5990-	130	1.6530	1.5330	19,992
Sep	1.6112	1.6122	1.5906	1.5968-	130	1.6480	1.5410	17,117
Dec	1.5900	1.5910	1.5980	1.5920-	130	1.6440	1.5500	177

Est vol 12,033; vol Wed 20,672; open int 37,287, +1,213.

	Open	High	Low	Settle	Change	Lifetime High	Low	Open Interest
Canadian Dollar (CME) - 100,000 dlrs.; $ per Can $								
June	.7250	.7278.	.7247	.7251+	.0013	.7600	.6948	13,404
Sep	.7222	.7261	.7222	.7234+	.0014	.7438	.6930	21,014
Dec	.7239	.7240	.7220	.7220+	.0015	.7400	.6895	2,234
Mr96	.7235	.7235	.7210	.7206+	.0016	.7355	.6900	1,047
June	.	....	....	.7192+	.0017	.7340	.6930	651

Est vol 4,470; vol Wed 8,415; open int 38,392, -2,423.

Exchange Rates
Thursday, June 15, 1995

The New York foreign exchange selling rates below apply to trading among banks in amounts of $1 million and more, as quoted at 3 p.m. Eastern time by Bankers Trust Co., Dow Jones Telerate Inc. and other sources.Retail transactions provide fewer units of foreign currency per dollar.

	U.S. $ equiv.		Currency per U.S. $	
Country	Thu	Wed	Thu	Wed
Argentina (peso)	1.0003	1.0001	.9997	.9999
Australia (Dollar)	.7274	.7215	1.3749	1.3861
Austria (Schilling)	.1008	.1017	9.9195	9.8355
Bahrain (Dinar)	2.6524	2.6524	.3770	.3770
Belgium (Franc)	.03462	.03481	28.886	28.724
Brazil (Real)	1.1044	1.1031	.9077	.9065
Britain (Pound)	1.5995	1.6115	.6252	.6205
30-day Forward	1.5991	1.6119	.6254	.6204
90-day Forward	1.5974	1.6102	.6260	.6210
180-day Forward	1.5931	1.6058	.6277	.6228
Canada (Dollar)	.7258	.7245	1.3778	1.3803
30-day Forward	.7252	.7231	1.3788	1.3829
90-day Forward	.7242	.7220	1.3809	1.3850
180-day Forward	.7229	.7205	1.3834	1.3879

continued on next page.

---

continued from previous page.

Comparative selections from two tables of currency quotations from the *Wall Street Journal* reveal the major differences between the interbank market and the futures markets. The rates quotes were for 3:00 P.M. EST, when the currency futures markets close. Exchange rates of the interbank are quoted both directly and indirectly, whereas most futures prices are quoted directly. The first price quoted for each currency under Exchange Rate is the spot bid price. It is referred to as a selling rate, since the bid is for dollars. Note that the quotes pertain to amounts of $1 million or more, and lesser (retail) amounts are bid lower.

The last trading date for September futures is September 18th, almost the precise value date of the 90-day forwards on June 15th. This illustrates the high correlation between futures and interbank rates. The September futures settling prices of .7234 (Canadian dollars) and 1.5968 (British pounds) are almost identical to the corresponding 90-day forwards. The most important difference concerns the method of dating. Unlike futures, the value date of the 90-day forward will always be 90 days away from spot. If the forward were bought or sold on June 15th, the resulting contract would continue to be priced almost identically to the September futures as both age toward settlement.

Servicing the Client

This is the one area of foreign currency management where a knowledgeable currency advisor can stand head and shoulders above the rest. Most of your competitors do not provide adequate service in risk management. Some do. Some major banks, for example, may have relationships with large multinationals that are unassailable. Also, some banks, both major and regional, are looking at mid-sized corporations as the next prime market for risk management services. Those who develop sound sales strategies will be formidable competitors; however, they will still be the exception to the rule.

Multinational Corporations

Assume the treasurer of a large multinational corporation wants to update its foreign currency program. The company has tens of millions of dollars of foreign exchange exposure in Asia, Latin America, and Europe. Where does the treasurer turn for help? His first call might be to a major bank headquartered, say, in New York, Chicago, or San Francisco. A customer relationship with this bank may already exist. The bank's foreign exchange department will be anxious to help, and can field an army of specialists toward this end. Since the bank's dealers have access to the interbank, and thus to virtually every tradable currency in the world, the treasurer can be assured of market access to the particular currencies in which his corporation is exposed. He may be hedging millions of dollars worth of currencies at a time, and the bank's transaction costs for these volumes are very competitive.

Will you be able to compete with this particular bank for this particular prospect? Probably not, but now let's turn to another example.

The Mid-sized Manufacturer

Able, Inc., a hypothetical U.S. corporation, manufactures laser surgical tools. It has built a strong market niche for itself in the United States, and is now venturing overseas. A few years ago it opened a distributorship in Canada, last year, one in England and, through a dealer network, it is beginning to sell medical equipment to various hospitals on the European continent. It also is planning to open a distributorship in Mexico City. The company's total annual sales last year were about $45 million.

Able's distributors order inventory several months in advance, and Able invoices them in the distributor's currency. The company usually has outstanding foreign currency receivables of several hundred thousand dollars, mostly denominated in Canadian dollars and British pounds. The treasurer wants to manage the company's foreign currency exposure better. He calls his local bank, which has an international business department, and has helped them in the past with letters of credit, export financing, and international shipping documents.

The manager of the international business department takes the call and, after listening to the treasurer's request, confesses that he knows very little about trading foreign currencies. He will find out and get back to him.

Later that afternoon, the bank loan officer handling the Able account calls the treasurer. "What's this about speculating in foreign currency?" he asks. The treasurer patiently explains that he is interested in hedging the company's foreign exchange exposure-not speculating. The loan officer says he will find out the bank's procedures for this, and get back to him. The next day, he again calls the treasurer, informs him he has gotten the information from the foreign exchange department (located at the main office on the other side of the state) and sets up an appointment.

If Able's treasurer expects to receive advice during this meeting on exposure management, he is quite disappointed. It turns out that the sole purpose of the meeting is to review the current financial status of the company. This is necessary, it is explained, to set up a foreign exchange line of credit. The bank officer is somewhat hazy about the size of line required, but decides that it will depend on the financials. He is also short of answers on exactly how to hedge currencies, but he assures the treasurer that the foreign exchange department will be happy to assist him. At the end of the meeting, the treasurer is given the phone number of the bank's dealing desk, and one last cautionary notice that "you can lose your shirt in this game."

Some time later, the treasurer decides to hedge a C$200,000 purchase order recently submitted by the Canadian distributor. He calls the foreign exchange desk of the bank. Introducing himself to the person who answers, he asks what the Canadian dollar is doing. "Are you buying or selling Canadian?" demands the dealer. The treasurer says he's buying. The dealer, realizing she is talking to a new customer, takes time to spell it out. "The bid is 3945 in a fast market." The treasurer asks about limit and stop orders. "We don't do those. The bid is 3945, good for fifteen seconds."

The treasurer buys, not knowing the cost of the transaction. (For one-fifth of a standard million dollar lot, it's substantial). Thinking that he has established a relationship with the dealer, he calls her back a week later for a market update. He is unaware that there are five dealers on the desk, who are always busy dealing. Some one else answers the phone. The treasurer introduces himself, and the dealer says, "Who?"

The Alternative

Admittedly, the above example is not the best-case scenario, but it is not highly unusual either. It comes down to a simple point. Most bankers are not traders. Their careers have developed in a highly risk-averse environment. The bank's primary function is to lend and borrow money in the most risk-free fashion possible. Bankers, in general, do not like to see their customers "gambling in foreign currencies."

Even within the securities industry, brokers face off across a communication gap separating the concepts of "speculation" and "investment." Consider, then, the language barrier within the banking industry between the bank's corporate loan officer and its foreign exchange dealer! Yet, both are required participants in a foreign exchange relationship, one to service the account, the other to transact the business. It is somewhat akin to a compliance officer joining forces with a scalper in the pits to prospect for clients. Probably neither will fully relate to the clients' needs, nor to each others'!

There is, of course, an alternative for Able's corporate treasurer. He can turn to a financial professional who understands both risk management *and* trading. Someone who can help him with both Asian and European currency exposures. Someone who can knowledgeably keep him informed about the currency market in general, including the

Mexican peso and any other currency in which the company may some-day have exposure. Someone who can help him transact through a variety of order executions, thereby selecting the most appropriate one at the time. Someone who fully discloses transaction costs up front, every time, and does not trade "against" the client. We're talking, of course, about you, representing the bank, the brokerage firm, or some other financial service provider—the foreign exchange management advisor.

Many banks and brokerage firms have access to either the interbank or the exchange-traded currency pits or both. Yet, only a few intrepid professionals are enjoying the lion's share of this business with mid-sized corporations. Why? They take the business by default. *No one else is calling.*

Basic Concepts of Foreign Exchange

What does the word "currency" really mean? According to John Stuart Mill, a currency:

... is a machine for doing quickly and commodiously, what would be done, though less quickly and commodiously, without it . . ."[1]

In other words, the function of money is to be a medium of exchange. Qualities that are important for a medium of exchange include being a standard unit of account and a store of value. These qualities are being compromised as currencies the world over have moved from specie to redeemability and then to fiat money (legal tender). Someone acquires something of value by exchanging units of currency for it. For a currency unit to be accepted in exchange, it must have value and the value must be maintained while the currency is held, unless the government mandates that it be accepted as payment for debt, which it does through legal tender laws. If the government debases the fiat currency over time through fiscal irresponsibility, the "medium of exchange" function does not change even in the medium term—it cannot because the government has made the fiat currency legal tender for "all debts public and private." (In the long term, as the German hyper-inflation of the 1920s showed, even this function may be compromised.) Yet the standard unit of account changes (it is no longer standard) as the currency is inflated (loses value as compared with other goods); thus, this quality has been compromised. What of the store of value? Obviously, a fiat currency cannot be considered a long-term store of value at all. Its value is entirely determined by what the issuing government says and does. In fact, economist Ludwig von Mises is reported to have said, "Government is the only body which can take a valuable commodity such as paper, put some ink on it and make it totally worthless."

Some currencies have other attributes. They may be "freely held," for example. (Not all are.) They may be "investable," or invested for profit. They may be easily and freely convertible into other currencies. *Reserve currencies*—those with which national governments choose to hold their foreign reserves—have these features, as do most other so-called "hard" currencies. The U.S. dollar is still the leading reserve currency, which means it is usually the first choice of most governments for denominating foreign reserves; however, this leading role has been contested for some time, with the Deutsche mark and Japanese yen being the main contestants.

Types of Currencies

Basically, there are three types of currencies. The first is *specie*, which is the term for money coined from precious metal (gold or silver). It most readily meets the requirements for relatively stable value because it is limited by nature. It is the most exchangeable and convertible of all currencies because the value of the precious metal from which it is struck is universally recognized and accepted.

The second type is a commodity-backed or redeemable currency. This most often takes the form of paper notes backed by gold or silver. The United States has had both silver and gold standards at various times in the past. To the degree that paper money is readily convertible at a ratio of one to one into the metal that backs it, a commodity-backed currency also has a relatively stable value. This type of currency is riskier to hold than specie because its convertibility depends on the issuer making good its promise to redeem the paper for the commodity that backs it.

The third type is *fiat* currency, which is an unbacked paper currency. It is considered to be currency only because the issuer mandates it to be legal tender. In other words, creditors are compelled by law to accept it in payment of any debt. There are three properties common to fiat currency:[2]

1. The currency is intrinsically worthless. It is a piece of paper (with a number on it).

2. It is unbacked. It carries no promise of redemption for anything other than another piece of paper.

3. It is virtually costless to produce, or at least whatever it is exchanged for is worth more than the production cost of the currency. Also the cost to produce 10 units of currency is virtually the

same as the cost to produce 100 units—the difference is a larger number on the paper.

Because it has no intrinsic value, fiat currency is considered by some financial scholars to be "price indeterminate" (the value cannot be determined or predicted mathematically); thus, it is subject to constant price analysis. This is the major challenge of foreign currency management because every industrialized country and most developing countries use fiat currency for domestic and international trading purposes.

All exchange-traded currencies today are fiat currencies. Their values are market determined and re-determined each day. Of course, in this respect they are no different from any other basic commodity, for which price is a function of supply and demand. As a futures broker, the best way to deal with currency contracts is to consider them to be like contracts in oats, porkbellies, and copper. Then we can better understand why the rest of the world has such a difficult time making sense of their apparently random changes in value.

Exchange Rate Determination

The U.S. dollar "floats." It was cut adrift (like the Mexican peso in the last days of 1994), to be priced by market forces. Floating the dollar is a relatively recent experiment. The dollar and the peso were allowed to float for essentially the same reason: the Fed and the Bank of Mexico had printed too many dollars and pesos, respectively. Until 1971, the dollar was fixed in value as a commodity-based currency. It could be exchanged upon demand for 1/35th of an ounce of gold. This convertibility underpinned the industrialized world's exchange arrangement known as the *Bretton Woods* system. Within this system, the major currencies were fixed in dollar value; hence, all currencies were, in a sense, tied to gold. In 1971, President Nixon declared that the dollar was not redeemable in gold because an international run on the U.S. gold supply was in full swing at the time (1/35th of an ounce of gold apparently was perceived as having more worth than $1). This action effectively ended the Bretton Woods system.

The current "independent float" of the dollar illustrates one system of determining exchange rates. Bretton Woods was another. The European Rate Mechanism (ERM) is yet another system. Both Bretton Woods and the ERM are known as "pegged" systems, in which the participating currencies are pegged to one another or to an outside standard, such as the

U.S. dollar, an inflation index, or a basket of currencies. The flexibility of pegged systems vary in regard to parity. Some currencies, such as the Hong Kong dollar and the Argentina peso, are rigidly fixed by a 'currency board.' In essence, the pegged currency can be readily redeemed for another, in this case, the U.S. dollar, held in reserve for that purpose. One is a proxy for the other. The ultimate step in this process is demonstrated by the Euro, the forthcoming European currency, which first pegs, then replaces the currencies within the system.

The exchange-traded currencies, like those of most trade-oriented countries, trade freely. They all float, either independently or in a group of sorts, in relation to the rest of the world, but none of these currencies float independently of governmental interference. Rather, they are "watched over" or managed to some degree by the central banks. Many so-called "floating" currencies are pegged in one fashion or another through bilateral or multilateral agreements.

Countries will often peg their local currency to a major currency to "protect" its value. The process of "pegging" constitutes a pledge that the government will do what is necessary to keep the value of its currency at a specific rate, or within specific rate boundaries of the stronger currency. Effectively, this constitutes a promise that it will debase its currency no faster than the one to which it is pegged is being debased, on average. Pegging one currency to another also facilitates trade between the countries by reducing the foreign exchange risk.

Exchange Rate Regimes

Like the governments that invoke them, exchange systems rise, hold sway for a while, and then disappear. They are distinguished primarily by the degree of flexibility, or inflexibility, in the determination of currency value. The International Monetary Fund (IMF) has defined seven broad classifications, or regimes, in which exchange rates are determined.[3] These are listed below from the least to the most flexible.

- *Single Currency Peg*—The central bank pegs to a major currency with infrequent adjustment of the parity. Many developing countries have used single currency pegs, but find they are difficult to defend when inflation and interest rates begin to deviate between the two currencies. The U.S. dollar and the French franc are most commonly used as pegs.

- *Composite Currency Peg*—The central bank pegs to a basket of currencies of major trading partners to make the pegged currency more stable than if a single currency peg were used. The weights assigned to the currencies in the basket may reflect the geographical distribution of trade, services, or capital flows. They may also be standardized, such as SDRs and ECUs.

- *Limited Flexibility vis à vis a Single Currency*—The value of the currency is maintained within a certain range of the peg (for example, Saudi Arabia's riyal peg to the U.S. dollar). There is also a core Deutsche mark block within the European Monetary System (EMS) which has more restrictive boundaries. This arrangement consists of the Deutsche mark, Swiss franc, Dutch guilder, and Belgian franc. The guilder and Belgian franc generally maintain a higher degree of correlation with the Deutsche mark. The Swiss franc, being an actively traded currency in its own right, correlates with the Deutsche Mark to a lesser extent.

- *Limited Flexibility through Cooperative Arrangements*—This applies to countries in the Exchange Rate Mechanism of the EMS and is a cross between a peg of individual EMS currencies to each other and a float of all these currencies jointly *vis à vis* non-EMS currencies (discussed below).

- *Greater Flexibility through Adjustment to an Indicator*—The currency is adjusted more or less automatically to changes in selected indicators. A common indicator is the true effective exchange rate, which reflects inflation-adjusted changes in the currency *vis à vis* major trading partners.

- *Greater Flexibility through a Managed Float*—The central bank sets the rate but varies it frequently. Indicators for adjusting the rate include, for example, the balance of payments position, reserves, and the parallel market developments. Adjustments are not automatic.

- *Full Flexibility through an Independent Float*—Rates are determined by market forces. Some industrial countries, as mentioned above, float their currencies within this regime. The number of developing countries in this category has been increasing in recent years.

Source: IMF Survey, October 26, 1992

Exchange Restrictions

Oftentimes, a central bank will attempt to support the price of its currency by restricting its convertibility in some fashion. Such exchange restrictions are especially tempting if the official rate of the currency can not be justified by the economics of the country. Rates might be controlled for a number of specific purposes. A central bank may want to keep its currency highly valued at home, but valued lower abroad for competitive reasons, or it may want to maintain a higher currency rate for international borrowings, to promote foreign capital investment, or to defend its international reserves. In any event, if a currency cannot be easily converted, it cannot be freely traded, so its rate is not subject to the whims of the market place.

Exchange restrictions affect the availability of a currency and, consequently, its value. A currency may be officially priced by making it unavailable at a lower rate of exchange that more truly reflects its value. As a result, *parallel markets* (a euphemism for black markets) often exist when there are exchange restrictions. These markets, though limited in scope due to risk of government prosecution, exchange currencies at rates more closely related to economic conditions.

There are many forms of exchange restrictions; for example, payments of current transactions for consumer imports may be unduly delayed. There may be multiple exchange rates, with some transactions taking place at market rates and others at higher "official" rates. Governments can be rather creative in this regard. Some of the rates devised for controlling the currency are:

- Agricultural product rate
- Commercial rate
- Controlled rate
- Essential import rate
- Export rate
- Financial rate
- Floating tourist rate
- Nonessential import rate
- Preferential rate
- Public transaction rate
- Priority rate

There may be cost-related import surcharges (as opposed to product-related tariffs). Some countries require advance import deposits or repatriation fees; or the rate of exchange is allowed to float freely against some currencies and not others. A selective float of the currency can be effected by bilateral payment arrangements between two countries that are not available to others. Sometimes foreign exchange or convertibility of the currency is forbidden at any price. The IMF has identified four examples of the multiple currency practices in common use today:[4]

Examples of Multiple Currency Practices

Dual or Multiple Market System—Multiple markets often consist of an official market in which the supply and demand for foreign exchange associated with certain specified transactions are controlled, and a free market that handles all other transactions. The free rate is almost always lower than the official rate. Less selective in their impact than the imposition of individual rates for given transactions, multiple markets typically penalize broad categories of suppliers of foreign exchange to the official market—usually exporters-and subsidize groups of purchasers—such as the government or special interest groups.

Fixed Exchange Rate on Given Transactions—Specific foreign exchange transactions can be either subsidized or penalized by the authorities, forcing the purchase or sale of exchange at an over- or undervalued exchange rate. Fixing the rate on certain transactions is often practiced to hold down official expenditures on the servicing of government-guaranteed debt, to encourage migrant labor, to repatriate foreign earnings, or to penalize profit remittances abroad by foreign companies or travel abroad by residents.

Taxes or Subsidies on the Value of Transactions—Similar in impact to fixing the exchange rate for given transactions, and equally selective, these practices typically target current account transactions. Examples include export bonuses or subsidies, mandatory advance import deposits (which pay no interest or less-than-market rates of interest), taxes on remittances abroad, and taxes on foreign exchange sales by commercial banks.

Excessive Spreads—Multiple currency practices result when the central bank prescribes buying and selling rates for spot foreign exchange transactions with a spread of more than 2% from their midpoint rate.

Source: Developments in International Exchange and Payments Systems, IMF

Appendix 3 contains a listing of currencies (some countries use more than one), along with their exchange rates as of a certain date in U.S. dollar units.

Purchasing Power

The fundamental process in determining the exchange rate of a freely traded currency is still not well understood—which is no surprise. The value of any freely-traded commodity is purely subjective. Theories for valuation abound, but the oldest theory is still the most widely used. It had its beginnings in sixteenth century Spain, and has been used in one form or another to this day. It forms the foundation for many more-modern schools of thought. It is the theory of *purchasing power parity*, often abbreviated "PPP." It states that the price of one currency, as defined in units of another, is determined by the level of prices in the one country as compared with the level of prices in the other.

Specifically, the PPP theory predicts that, everything being equal, a basket of goods that moves freely across borders must eventually cost the same wherever it is sold. The driving force is competition. If a disparity in prices between two countries begins to grow, competitive pressures will soon cause the disparity to disappear. Goods and money flow in opposite directions across the currency border until price equilibrium is again achieved.

Assume that there are two currencies, designated HC (home currency) and FC (foreign currency). A basket of consumer goods, perhaps a sampling of food staples, textiles, and energy products, trades freely between the countries of these currencies. Imagine, now, that in the HC country, this basket costs 500 HC units. In the FC country, the same basket costs 1,000 FC units. We can deduce that one HC unit is worth about two FC units.

Our deducement is correct if the two currencies are at parity in purchasing power. If this were *not* the correct exchange rate, according to the theory, *arbitrageurs* would see that there was an automatic profit to be made by exchanging goods across the border until either the prices or the exchange rate fell into line. In reality, of course, the basket is a proxy for *all* the goods and services in one country compared to *all* the goods and services in the other.

The theory is expressed by the following equation:

$$hc/fc = P\ hc\ /P\ fc$$

where:
  hc/fc is the exchange rate,
  P hc is the price of goods in home currency and
  P fc is the price of goods in foreign currency.

Using this equation:
  hc/fc = 500/1000 (or 0.50), where 500 and 1000 equal the prices of the respective baskets.

Figure 3-1

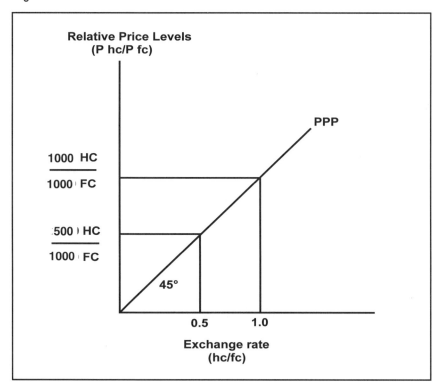

Source: *Purchasing Power Parity*, Merrill Lynch, 1990

Purchasing power parity can be diagrammed as a function of exchange rates and relative price levels. Figure 3-1 shows PPP as a 45° line measuring two variables: exchange rate and basket price. At every point on the line, the equation $hc/fc = P\,hc\,/P\,fc$ holds true, as relative price levels and the exchange rate move in direct proportion to one another. If, for example, our basket goes from 500 HC to 1000 HC, while remaining unchanged at 1000 FC, the change in relative prices would cause the exchange rate to adjust from .50 to 1.00.

As popular as it is, the theory of PPP has a major problem. Namely, it does not accurately predict variations in exchange rates. In fact, over the years, there have been large and persistent departures from the expected relative price levels and exchange rate levels, both long-term and short-term. The theory can hardly be relied on for making major currency decisions. It certainly cannot be used as a stand-alone forecasting indicator. Purchasing power parity theory can only *suggest* relationships. There are several reasons for this imprecision. One is the restrictions placed on exchange rates. Another is the restrictions placed on the free flow of goods, such restrictions as tariffs and transportation costs. Also, it is difficult to construct a basket of goods that actually has the same perceived value, and therefore the same supply and demand characteristics, from one country to another. Lastly, mathematical models can never precisely match the aggregate of all the *subjective valuations* taking place in the market.

Nevertheless, PPP seems to become a factor over a span of several years. It has been well documented that prices of goods, services, and currencies tend to move toward equilibrium. This tendency may become even more pronounced in the current environment in which tariffs and other trade barriers are breaking down. The Mexican peso in early 1995 is a good example of this tendency.

Real and Nominal Rates

Interest rates have a major impact on relative currency values. Two types of interest rates that are helpful in understanding exchange rates are real and nominal interest rates.

Figure 3-2: PPP and Arbitrage

The tendency of currencies to gravitate toward Purchasing Power Parity through arbitrage can be shown by visualizing goods and currencies as units of value. Assume that the currency "HC" can purchase 100% of a basket of goods "BG," and that "HC" is equal to "FC." Assume also that "FC" can purchase 110% of the same basket. This sets up a "three-point arbitrage situation," so called because it involves three separate transactions. Place all three units arbitrarily in a circle, and connect them with a directional arrow of transaction. If the arrow can be made to generate a profit in one direction (with a loss in the other), automatic profits can occur from arbitrage.

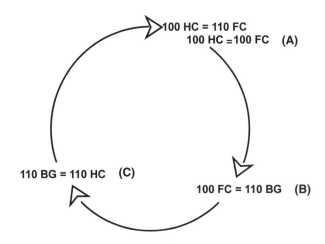

100 HC = 110 FC
100 HC = 100 FC   **(A)**

110 BG = 110 HC   **(C)**

100 FC = 110 BG   **(B)**

In this case, a trader swaps 100 HC for 100 FC (A), then buys 110 BG (B) which she sells for 110 HC (C). The circle continues to spin profitably as 110 HC is swapped for 110 FC, 110 FC is swapped for 121 BG, etc. Arbitrage activity sows the seeds of its own destruction through the laws of supply and demand. The continuous demand for FC purchases with HC will raise the price of FC relative to the price of HC until the trading profits disappear.

If "BG" were another currency rather than a basket of physical goods, the transactions could take place immediately at insignificant cost. This is why market arbitrage occurs instantly and parity is achieved within minutes. Our example, however, involves the costs of trading goods, including transportation, distribution, and so forth. These costs must be made economical before arbitrage can take place. For this reason, Purchasing Power Parity is usually achieved, if ever, only in a very long time frame.

The difference between nominal interest rates and real interest rates has to do with the rate of inflation. If $100 earns $10 in one year, the per annum interest rate is 10%. That is the nominal rate. If there were zero inflation, 10% would also be the real rate of interest. If, however, inflation averaged 4% for the year, the real interest rate would be only 6%. The real rate, in other words, is what you *really* earn on your savings after considering the effects of inflation.

By the same token, an understanding of Purchasing Power Parity helps to distinguish between nominal and real exchange rate *changes*. Consider the following value change over a period of time:

Start of period	*End of period*
100 HC = 100 FC	100 HC = 110 FC

We see a change in *nominal* rates. Nominal rate changes result in the fluctuating market values that occur every day; however, the market does not tell us whether or not there is a change in the *real* exchange rate. A real rate of exchange refers to the comparative values of two currencies at purchasing power parity, which means no arbitrage opportunities exist. A change in real rates, therefore, implies a change in purchasing power parity. If the nominal rate and the real rate do not change to the same degree, PPP no longer exists. A change in the real rates of exchange may result from a relative change in inflation rates between the two countries. If the nominal rate does not keep pace, the increase in inflation is not yet fully discounted by the market. Disparities in moves between nominal and real rates can also be caused by inducing a currency value change outside the market, perhaps by raising interest rates or restricting the currency's convertibility.

Consider the following examples in which we apply the basket of goods from the theory of PPP.

7/1/97	**7/1/98**
100 HC = 1 BG	100 HC = 1 BG
100 FC = 1 BG	110 FC = 1 BG
100 HC = 100 FC	100 HC = 110 FC
Base rate	Change in PPP Matches
	Nominal Rate Change
	Therefore, No Change in Real Rate

Over the period of a year, the relative levels of purchasing power remained the same. The new exchange rate of 1.10 still allows us to swap one currency for the other without a loss (or gain) in purchasing power. Because the change in PPP is reflected in the change in nominal rates, the real exchange rate remains as is. According to the PPP theory, if purchasing power (i.e., relative inflation rates) changes, the nominal rate must change to regain parity and to maintain the real rate of exchange. Likewise, if the currency rate changes first, a change in purchasing power must follow if a change in real rates is not going to occur.

Remember that *any* change in the exchange rate is, by definition, a change in the nominal rate. As shown above, when the move compensates *precisely* for a change in relative purchasing power, *only* the nominal rate changes. Let's compare the above example with the following:

7/1/97	**7/1/98**
100 HC = 1 BG	100 HC = 1 BG
100 FC = 1 BG	100 FC = 1 BG
100 HC = 100 FC	100 HC = 110 FC
Base Rate	Nominal Rate Change but
	No PPP Change
	Therefore, Change in Real Rate

Any portion of a nominal rate change that does not represent an identical change in purchasing power represents a change in real exchange rates. In this example, therefore, both nominal and real rates have changed. Under different conditions, a change in the real rate can occur while the nominal rate remains constant, as shown below:

7/1/97	**7/1/98**
100 HC = 1 BG	100 HC = 1 BG
100 FC = 1 BG	110 FC = 1 BG
100 HC = 100 FC	100 HC = 100 FC
Base Rate	PPP Change but
	No Nominal Rate Change
	Therefore, Change in Real Rate

During the year, FC depreciated. It now takes 110 FC to buy the same basket of goods that could be bought for 100 FC one year earlier. There is no compensating change in nominal exchange rates (100 HC still equals 100 FC). The net result is an approximate 10% change in real exchange rates. This commonly occurs when the exchange rate is "stuck," perhaps at an official rate. The economics surrounding the currency may change, but the rate remains the same. To maintain this nominal rate, stringent exchange controls sometimes are put into effect which prevent the currency from trading at a more realistic price.

The example below shows a common occurrence with freely traded currencies:

7/1/89	7/1/91	7/1/97
100 HC = 1 BG	100 HC = 1 BG	100 HC = 1 BG
100 FC = 1 BG	110 FC = 1 BG	115 FC = 1 BG
100 HC = 100 FC	100 HC = 120 FC	100 HC = 115 FC
Base Rate	Change in Nominal and Real Rates	Change in Nominal Rate Only

As illustrated here, the FC economy experienced 10% inflation between 1989 and 1991. In 1991, it takes 110 FC to purchase 1 BG, which cost 100 FC in 1989. During this time, HC economy's inflation rate was 0%, and there has been a nominal rate change of 20%. The difference between the nominal rate change and the relative inflation rates constitutes a real exchange rate change. Purchasing power parity no longer exists.

Over a longer period of time (five to ten years), real rate changes tend to balance each other out as PPP is regained. In our example, the real rate variance disappears by 1997, when PPP is restored. Recent history shows that most commonly, in the near term, volatility in both real and nominal rates of exchange is a daily occurrence.

Interest Rate Parity

Let's say that a U.S. engineering corporation purchases new road-building equipment from a manufacturer located in an FC country. The manufacturer sells the equipment for 1,000,000 FC, with payment due one year from the date of sale. The corporate treasurer now has an FC payable on the books and is concerned about the exposure. He decides to hedge this liability, and looks at two options (assume FC futures trade on an exchange and the current FC/$ spot rate is 1.00):

1 The treasurer can immediately exchange $1,000,000 for 1,000,000 FC and invest the foreign currency. (To eliminate extraneous risk factors, let's say he invests in a money market instrument comparable to a U.S. treasury bill.) The FC payment is due when the instrument matures.

2 He can purchase FC one-year forward or futures contracts, take delivery when the contracts mature, and make the payment. (Alternatively, of course, he can liquidate the contract, take the gain or loss, and apply it toward the purchase of spot FC.) Note that a third alternative, borrowing FC and investing it for one year, doesn't work in this instance because it merely substitutes one FC liability for another.

The treasurer looks for the most economical option and discovers that all are virtually equal in cost, as shown by the following:

Value Date of FC	Exchange Rate ($/FC)	Interest Rate (one-year)
spot	1.00 ($1.00 = 1.00 FC)	$ = 10%
one-year forward	1.05 ($1.05 = 1.00 FC)	FC = 5%

With the first option, the treasurer foregoes the interest for one year on dollars (10%), and earns one year of interest on FC (5%). This represents a net cost equal to 5% of $1,000,000. With the second option, he earns 10% on $1,000,000 for the year because he doesn't trade it for FC; however, he pays a premium for the one-year futures, which costs 5% in dollar terms. Again, the net cost is 5% of $1,000,000.

This "one is the same as the other" result applies in every case. This correlation is known as *interest rate parity*. The correlation works in both directions. If the interest rate were 10% for FC, and 5% for dollars, the futures would be discounted from the spot, rather than priced at a premium. Let's look at this scenario:

Value Date of FC	Exchange Rate ($/FC)	Interest Rate (one year)
spot	1.00 ($1.00 = 1.00 FC)	$ = 5%
one-year forward	.95 ($0.95 = 1.00 FC)	FC = 10%

Now, the cost becomes a gain, but again, the amount is the same, regardless of which option is chosen. With the first option, the treasurer can gain 5% by converting dollars to FC and investing it at 10% for a year, foregoing a 5% earning on dollars, or he can gain the same 5% by purchasing forwards or futures at a discount.

Does the company actually realize a gain by hedging in discount currencies? Probably not. Remember that the treasurer starts out with an FC liability. He is seeking to eliminate the exchange risk it represents by acquiring an FC asset in one form or another. The discounted purchasing price of the futures (the asset) more than likely will be offset by the higher interest cost factored into the payable. By the same token, the 5% "cost" in the first example is offset by the lower interest rate charged for the liability.

The terms *premium currency* (futures priced at a premium to spot) and *discount currency* (futures priced at a discount to spot) are used to identify which currency has the higher or lower yield. By knowing either the futures price or the interest rate, the other can be approximated out to about a year distant. The calculations are less exact as the time frame gets longer than that because other risks come into play. Even so, forward contracts out as far as twenty years are not unknown.

An underlying assumption of the Interest Rate Parity theory is that the foreign currency interest rate is 0%. Obviously, this is never the case in a world of fiat currencies; however, the theory is still widely discussed. For those with a mathematical bent, calculation of Interest Rate Parity is shown in Figure 3-3.

The Fallacious "Hot Money" Theory

There is no doubt that interest rates and exchange rates have a profound effect upon each other; however, the relationship is not well understood. A popular misconception has to do with "hot money." Many believe that a huge source of funds overhangs the currency markets worldwide. Whenever interest rates rise in one country, especially a major industrial country with an unrestricted currency, the fund managers rush in to take advantage of the increased yield. Funds remain parked in that currency only until the rate of interest moves back down, or interest rates for other

Figure 3-3

Calculation of Interest Rate Parity

$$\frac{F}{S} \text{ @ } \frac{1 + R \text{ hc}}{1 + R \text{ fc}}$$

where F is the direct exchange rate of the one-year futures or forward; S is the direct exchange rate for spot; R hc is the one-year interest rate of the home currency (U.S. $, in this case), and R fc is the one-year interest rate of the foreign currency.

   Assume S = 100, R hc = .10 , and R fc = .05.
What is the approximate one-year futures or forward rate (F)?

$$\frac{F}{1.00} \text{ @ } \frac{1 + .10}{1 + .05} = 1.0477619$$

Therefore, F @ 1.047

Simply stated, the difference between the spot and futures or forward rates is approximately equivalent to the difference between the interest rates. For both sides to be precisely equal, both denominators would have to equal 1.00, which would only occur if the foreign currency interest rate were 0%—which never happens. The higher the foreign currency interest rate, the greater the error factor.

---

currencies move higher, at which time they again flow into the currency paying the highest yield. Proponents of the "hot money" theory contend that the sudden shifts in demand have a dramatic effect on exchange rates, with the highest yielding currency rising quickly in price as buyers pour in.

   With the very deep pockets of today's global fund managers, and with today's instant telecommunication and transfer capabilities, the "hot money" theory appears quite plausible; however, it is a false perception. There is no tremendous flow of funds chasing interest rates. Some money does, but not much, and "hot money" does not move exchange rates. This is because the implied automatic gains simply do not exist. The implication of automatic losses is just as valid.

A look at the treasurer's options reveals the problem. Remember that the higher interest-yielding currency trades at a discount. It has less value in the future. An investor who buys a currency at spot to capture an interest rate premium simply gives back the premium when he later sells the currency at a lower price.

Of course, there is a way to avoid selling at a discount. The investor can simply hold the currency unhedged, hoping that the forward price rises to the current spot level, but then it is no longer an interest rate game. The "hot money" investor chasing interest rate yield ends up speculating in foreign exchange, just like any other currency trader.

Why Interest Rate Parity?

Conventional wisdom has it that forward rates are determined by interest rate parity because of arbitrage. In other words, interest rate differentials translate into forward pricing, so any mis-price between the cash and forward markets is instantly traded away. Interest rate parity works, according to this line of reasoning, because arbitrage makes it work. But does it really? It is just as easy to argue that arbitrage is simply an effect of interest rate parity, rather than the cause. Perhaps *arbitrageurs* act quickly when noticing a price disparity only because they realize that parity will occur *regardless* of what they do. It can be shown that this is what actually happens, and that interest rate parity is much more fundamental than the results produced by arbitrage.

Imagine the following scenario: you are approached by a benefactor who proposes to enhance your well-being. He offers you $1,000 with no strings attached. You are given two choices. Either you can receive the cash immediately, or you can receive the cash after an interval of one year. Which option would you choose?

There is a high probability that you would take the cash immediately. Why? For the following reasons:

1. The delay of one year represents 365 days of lost opportunity. You can purchase a lot of things with $1,000 during a year's time (this is the time value of money).

2. The money will be less valuable in one year because of the effects of inflation.

3. The future is uncertain. The benefactor may change his mind or lose the money during the year.

In short, there are three factors which affect the value of money to be received in the future: the time value of money, the inflation rate, and the borrower's (or benefactor's) credit risk.

Although we cannot determine the future value of $1,000 today, we can measure precisely the *expected* future value. It is equal to the current inducement that must be paid to turn *money in hand* into *money promised*. Stated another way, the current value of a future sum of money is determined by the current rate of interest.

Viewed in this manner, we can neglect for the moment the differences between nominal and real interest rates. It is the nominal rate of interest, after all, that determines the price differential between spot and forward prices of nominal exchange rates. In fact, the two rates are simply different expressions of the same thing, as we illustrated in the foregoing Interest Rate Parity equation.

Figure 3-4

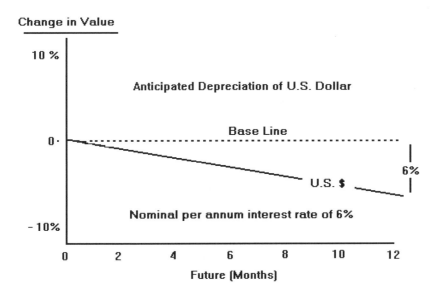

Figure 3-4 implies that the inducement to save one dollar for a certain period of time instead of spending it must equal the sum of the originary rate (derived from the time value of money), the inflation rate, and the credit risk during the same period of time. This is reflected in the nominal rate of interest. In this case, the inducement to save one U.S. dollar for one year is 6% of its current value. Another currency may require a greater or lesser inducement, on whether its anticipated depreciation is more or less that of the dollar. Figure 3-5 compares foreign currency x (FCx) to the dollar. It shows that FCx is anticipated to depreciate faster than the U.S. dollar, thereby requiring a greater inducement (nominal interest rate). Viewed another way, the forward value of FCx is discounted to that of the dollar.

Figure 3-5

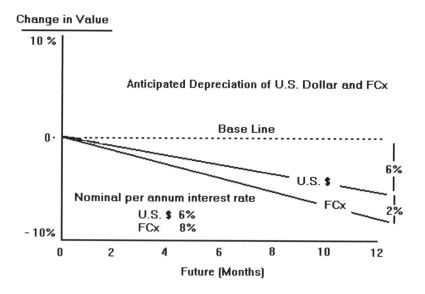

The implication of the relationship between currency depreciation, interest rates, and forward rates, allows us to try to develop a model to relate interest rates to forward rates. This model can be applied to compare the dollar with three hypothetical currencies. One is a specie currency designated "Gold $." The other two are foreign currencies, "FCa" and

"FCb." Exhibit 3-6 shows how these currencies compare in loss of value after one year.

Figure 3-6

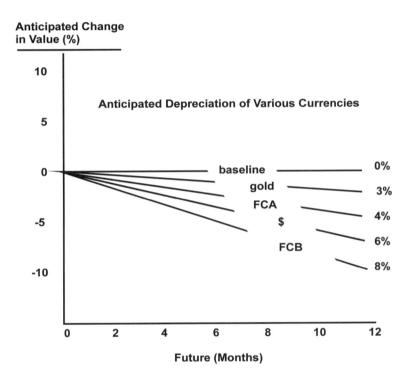

We can see from this chart that the nominal per annum rate of interest is 4% for FCa, 6% for the U.S. dollar, and 8% for FCb. Gold $ does not undergo *monetary* inflation, so the interest rate consists only of an originary rate and a credit risk premium, totaling 2%.

Now, consider the currencies *relative to the dollar*. Note that Gold $ and FCa are at a premium to the U.S.dollar, while FCb is at a discount. By using the U.S.dollar as the standard, all currencies with lower interest rates are rendered premium currencies, and all currencies with higher interest rates become discount currencies. Because the originary rate is small and constant, usually around 2-3%, and credit risk of governments is rarely called into question, the primary factor affecting interest rate levels is inflation. Thus, we would expect Gold $ and FCa to have lower inflation rates than the U.S.dollar and FCb to have a higher inflation rate.

Figure 3-7 shows the differentials between spot and forward exchange rates when real foreign currency values are measured against a nominal dollar value. Those who trade futures may recognize the forward price differential as the *cost of carry*. This cost usually consists of interest, insurance, and storage. Because currency holdings do not require payment of insurance or storage fees, the cost of carry is simply the difference between the rates of interest.

Figure 3-7

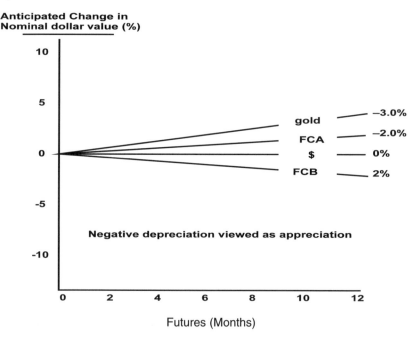

**Anticipated Change in
Nominal dollar value (%)**

Futures (Months)

With a world of fiat currencies being valued relative to the dollar, we can say that the nominal value of the dollar remains constant over time, while the real value may decline through inflation. In fact, this has been the case; thus, premium currencies are losing purchasing power more slowly than the dollar, while discount currencies are losing purchasing power more quickly than the dollar. The whole world is on a sliding scale.

The Eurorate

If we know that the difference between the spot and forward rates reflects the difference between the interest rate yield of the U.S. dollar and the foreign currency, the question becomes, "which interest rate?" Obviously, choosing an arbitrary rate of interest for one currency to compare with an arbitrary rate of interest for another would create an unreliable and inconsistent forward market. A universal standard is required. The market has chosen the *Eurorate*, a reasonable choice because this is the rate that the interbank applies to loans of foreign currency deposits.

Specifically, Eurorates are the interest rates one bank charges another to borrow foreign currency for the short term (overnight to one year). If the U.S. dollar is the foreign currency, the *Eurodollar* rate applies. If the foreign currency is the Japanese yen, the borrower is charged the *Euroyen* rate, if it is the Deutsche mark, the *Euromark* rate applies, and so forth. The terminology should be clarified. The Eurodollar is not an interest rate. It is the term used for a foreign currency deposit, in which the currency happens to be U.S. dollars. The rate charged for Eurodollars is the LIBOR, or the London Interbank Offered Rate. Eurodollars are lent at the LIBOR because the Eurorate market originated in London with U.S. dollar deposits.

You may notice little difference between the interbank currency forward market, in which foreign currency deposits are bought and sold on time, and the interbank Eurorate market, in which foreign currency deposits are lent and borrowed on time. There is, in fact, virtually no difference between these two markets. The variance between spot and forward is actually the difference between the LIBOR and the corresponding Eurorate. In fact, some dealer to dealer quotes for forward pricing involve simply quoting LIBOR plus or minus the points. The rest is extrapolated. We can summarize the interrelations between forward exchange rates and futures rates by stating:

The variance between spot and forward exchange rates for any two currencies equals the Eurorate variance of the currencies.

Effects of Interest Rate Changes

Because the difference between spot and forward pricing is simply an interest rate differential, is it possible to predict the change in forward rates if we're aware of a change in interest rates? If there were breaking news, one morning, that a central bank just increased its key overnight lending rate, would we know, *a priori*, whether the spot would change, or whether the forward rate would change, and how much of a change there would be?

The answer is a qualified no. We know definitely that the spot or the forward rate, or both, will react to regain interest rate parity; but we don't know which rate will bear the brunt of the change. It depends mostly on the market's perception of *why* the interest rate was increased. Assume that the central bank of "Red Ink Republic" raised its discount rate in an attempt to stabilize a weak currency that has been battered, of late, because of rising inflation. In response, the Eurorate goes from 7.5% to 8.0%. One of three possible market moves will take place, as shown in Figures 3-8, 3-9, and 3-10.

In all three cases shown in Figures 3-7, 3-8, and 3-9, we can predict, *a priori*, the change in value over time, but the change in relationship to the U.S. dollar is not as clear cut. In the case of "Red Ink Republic," scenario (A) may have been expected, but the market may react with scenario (C) instead, leading analysts to conclude that the central bank did not "go far enough." These scenarios illustrate the flaws of the "hot money" theory.

Figure 3-8

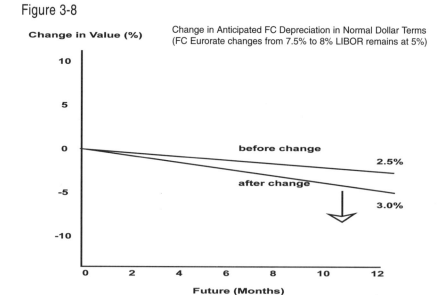

Scenario A: Market neutral to interest rate change. Major impact on forward rates, less impact on Spot.

Figure 3-9

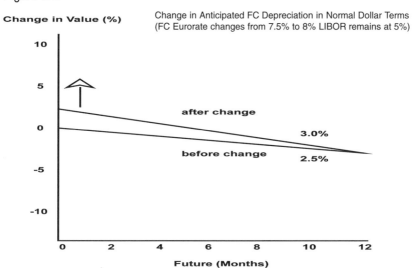

Scenario B: Market positive to interest rate change. Major impact on spot, less on forward rates.

Figure 3-10

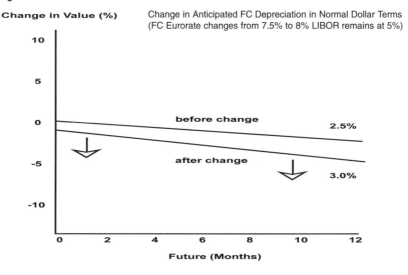

Scenario C: Market negative to interest rate change. Major impact on both spot and forward rates.

Basic Concepts of Hedging

Mid-sized corporations which are actively pursuing international opportunities are your key prospective clients. They probably already export or import out of or into nearby countries such as Canada and Mexico. They may be doing business in Europe. Perhaps they utilize the international capital market as investors or venture partners. In any event, these prospects are fully aware of the risks and pitfalls of dealing with foreign exchange, but do not have the expertise to manage them.

On a personal level, the prospect is the treasurer, the CFO, or the CEO of this corporation. You are likely to meet all three of them, probably in that order. If that is the case, the chances are good that the individual's foreign exchange knowledge *diminishes* as you progress from one to the next. In other words, the treasurer is in a "hands on" position, closely connected with the day-to-day market, and stays on top of the latest financial developments. The CFO, and especially the CEO, may have a much more general knowledge without being aware of the particulars; therefore, the treasurer, or someone acting in that capacity, should be your first "serious" contact.

Assume that you've done your homework and have a fairly good idea of the exposures impacting the company. Now you are sitting at a conference table with a financial officer who—as far as you know—has as much insight into foreign currency trading as you do. What are you going to talk to him about?

What is a Hedge?

No matter how the conversation begins, at some point you will be discussing the merits and techniques of hedging. Your risk management expertise, after all, is what brings you to the table; therefore, knowing this subject "cold" is absolutely required. Perhaps you do. If you are a futures broker, hedging may already be all or part of your business, be it in agriculture, energy, or finance. Or you may have a book that is strictly speculative and have never put on a hedge position. If you represent a bank or other financial institution, you may already have a good handle on financial instruments. Whatever the case, reviewing the basics of exposure management is worth the effort. Let's look at some of the building blocks—the hedging concepts—that you can build your presentation on.

The Long and the Short of It

The terms "long" and "short" are common knowledge. These terms are used daily to define market positions. To explain hedging to someone who is not familiar with it, it is advantageous to broaden these definitions substantially. Begin by classifying every corporate asset and liability, tangible or intangible, monetized or of undefined value, as a long or short position. If we can prod the treasurer, and ourselves, into thinking in these broad terms, the concept of hedging becomes much easier to grasp and to explain. *Longs* refer to the things we have. We are long assets. *Shorts* are the things we don't have, but are obligated in some way to acquire. Life itself is an ebb and flow into and out of long and short positions. We are long the house we live in, but short the mortgage. We are long the car, but short the bicycles we promised the kids for Christmas; or take a retail example: a car distributor starts out long cash and short cars. After purchasing inventory from the distributor, he is long cars and short cash. He gradually goes long cash and short cars again, and the cycle begins anew. (You may note that a third position of "not long," meaning that we don't have it and don't need it, is ignored here because it is not relevant.)

Besides cars and bicycles, intangibles can also be classified as longs and shorts. For example, a U.S. company competing in the domestic market against an import produced in Canada may have a long Canadian dollar exposure, even though it doesn't own a single Canadian dollar. It does, however, operate from a competitive position that benefits from a rise in the value of Canadian dollars. The Canadian firm, of course, has a long U.S. dollar exposure for the identical reason. We can say, therefore, that the U.S. firm is "long Canadian dollars" and the Canadian firm is "long U.S. dollars."

The positions of these two companies are exact opposites of each other. This illustrates an important principal concerning long and short positions. Any short position in *foreign currency* is the same as a long position in home currency, as it relates to the rate of exchange between the two. The converse, of course, is also true: a short position in *home currency* is a long position in a foreign currency. One does not exist without the other. The U.S. company, therefore, has a short U.S. dollar and long Canadian dollar position. The Canadian company has a long U.S. dollar and short Canadian dollar position.

Using this broad brush approach, we can define our terms of "long" and "short" as follows:

- A long position is anything that benefits the holder by an increase in value and adversely affects the holder by a decrease in value.

- A short position is anything that benefits the holder by a decrease in value and adversely affects the holder by an increase in value.

Equal but Opposite Positions

Consider the hypothetical foreign exchange account of Company ABC in Table 4-1.

Table 4-1: Company ABC FX Account

Date		Long	Short	Value Date
1 Feb.	Canadian dollar		2,000,000	1 Mar
1 Feb.	Swiss franc	4,000,000		1 Mar
15 Feb.	Canadian dollar	1,000,000		1 Mar
15 Feb.	Canadian dollar		2,000,000	15 Mar
15 Feb.	Swiss franc		2,000,000	15 Mar

What is the company's foreign exchange position? What is its foreign exchange exposure? These are two different things. Four positions exist in the account: (1) a 4,000,000 Canadian dollar short, (2) a 1,000,000 Canadian dollar long, (3) a 2,000,000 Swiss franc short, (4) a 4,000,000 Swiss franc long. (All forward positions remain open until the value date.) The company's *exposure*, however, is short 3,000,000 Canadian dollars and long 2,000,000 Swiss francs. The rest of the position is covered. In other words:

Equal but opposite (long and short) positions offset each other; creating an overall neutral position in which changes in value are balanced out.

Of course, this is elementary and well-understood by most traders, but not every one is a trader, including the prospective client; thus, a sales presentation may easily go over the heads of the prospective clients. It is a good rule of thumb to always cover the basics. Only by turning a few specific industry buzz words into visualizations can we make foreign currency management comprehensible to lay people. It is important for the prospect to know that, put simply, an exposure management program means hedging. It is important, then, to be very clear about what hedging means:

Hedging means offsetting a given position by taking a position of equal size and opposite direction. The effect of the offsetting position is to reduce or eliminate the effects of changes in the value of both positions.

Figure 4-1: A Canadian Dollar Hedge

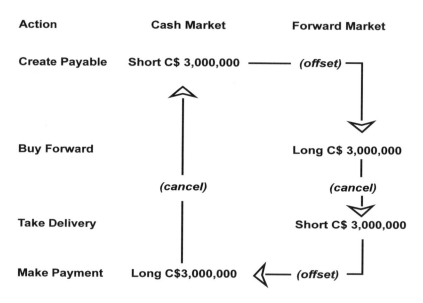

Long and short positions in different markets offset each other.
Long and short positions in the same market cancel each other out.

Transferring Risk

It is important that the prospect understands another basic principal: the transference of risk. Hedges do not *eliminate* exposures nor the risks they entail; they *transfer* them. This concept is at the core of any effective risk-management program. In fact, the failure to understand tranference is the major reason that recognized exposures are often unwittingly converted into unrecognized exposures. The principle of transference is not self-evident, and the question is often raised, "if the risk is transferred, who ends up with it?" The recipient depends solely on the strategy or method of hedging employed.

Hedger to Market Place

The tranference from the hedger to the market place occurs most often with operating exposure. The term "market place" means the economy of the local currency in which the company sells its product or service. There are, of course, many ways of refining this definition. A consumer-oriented company may consider the entire retail sector of a country as its market place; or the term may refer to a very specialized segment, such as a specific industry group. Toyota and Honda build automobile plants in the United States to transfer their long dollar exposures, and the attendant risks, to the U.S. auto worker. Those associated with the domestic auto industry happily accept the risk. If the dollar drops in value against the yen, the American consumer pays "cheaper" dollars to acquire a Japanese model, but also receives cheaper dollars to build it. Unless we are planning to retire in Japan, that value change is insignificant.

It becomes more significant, however, if U.S. dollars are used to buy Japanese imports. Consider what happens when an import is purchased, be it a car, a camera, or a forging press. Between the time the purchase is budgeted and the time it is paid for, a short foreign currency exposure is assumed. The price paid is directly influenced by the exchange rate between the home currency of the exporter and the local currency. The purchaser is "short" the car or the camera until it is paid for; in the same way, he is short the foreign currency expenditure that results in its production. It would be to his advantage, in a narrow financial sense, to see the foreign currency lose value.

Do U.S. residents really assume a foreign currency exposure—transferred by an overseas manufacturer who builds its automobiles in the United States? Technically, if a Japanese manufacturer initiates production of consumer products in this country, the consumers transfer their short yen exposure to the manufacturer while it transfers its long dollar exposure to the U.S. consumers. The dollar-based sticker price paid to own a Mazda out of Flat Rock, Michigan and the dollar-based profit to Mazda no longer depend on the price of yen-based labor in Japan. It now depends on the price of dollar-based labor in the midwest. Risks have been exchanged by transference of exposure in both directions. Currency mis-matches have been eliminated all the way around.

Hedger to Hedger

Let's assume your client has a liability of 100 million Mexican pesos in the form of a payable, due in two years. At this point in time, he doesn't have a peso to his name, so he is short 100 million Mexican pesos. He can transfer the risk several ways. One way is to enter the over-the-counter market and swap pesos for dollars on a two-year contract basis. The swap would be structured so that your client buys pesos from a counterparty, who buys dollars from him. Two years from now, when he pays off the liability, your client returns the pesos and the counterparty returns the dollars. In the meantime, your client realizes any gain in the exchange rate of the pesos, which offsets his liability exposure.

Because this client initiated the swap by buying pesos, the counterparty responds by selling them to him. In other words, the counterparty "shorts" pesos. In essence, it has accepted your client's short position; he transferred the risk of his exposure to the counterparty. A transference of risk through a currency swap is normally an exchange of positions between hedgers. In this example, the counterparty may be a U.S. company with a 100 million peso asset located in Mexico. Let's assume this asset must be liquidated and repatriated in U.S. dollars in two years. The company therefore has a long exposure in pesos. It accepts your client's short position, thereby offsetting both. In the process of assuming his short position, the counterparty transfers the risk of its long position to your client.

Hedger to Speculator

Now assume you have a client with a liability of 10,000,000 Canadian dollars, and a time span of six months. He decides to transfer the risk of this short position using futures contracts. An order is entered on the CME to buy 100 contracts of September Canadian dollars on the opening. This gives the hedger a long futures position which is equal in size and opposite in direction to his cash market exposure. The market opens and moves higher. Who is there to take his order? The local, the scalper, the spreader, or maybe another broker who does the trade for his client's speculative account. The futures market is the ideal arena for "hedger to speculator" risk transference. The speculator frequently accepts the risk in an attempt to make a profit, and the hedger is happy to hand the risk over to him. Unquestionably, the role of the speculator is essential to the liquidity and easy convertibility that characterizes the foreign exchange futures markets. Hedging would be extremely expensive and burdensome without it.

Hedger to Supplier

A starting point in the development of any hedge program is to determine whether financial hedges are actually necessary. Foreign exchange trading, even in the most carefully planned risk management program, is never a risk-free proposition. Without careful management, exposure risk may translate into even higher trading risk. If another way can be found to reduce exposure for the prospect, a broker or dealer may lose an immediate transaction fee, but gain a long-term client in return. One possibility that deserves consideration is transferring short exposures, such as deferred payables, to the supplier. There is no exposure when dealing strictly in the home currency. From the standpoint of a U.S. company, if purchase orders can be denominated in U.S. dollars, the risk of the exposure automatically transfers to the supplier. This is one of the easiest methods of managing foreign currencies.

Of course, this type of hedging is not always the most desirable, even when it is available. The supplier may not be willing to assume the exposure; his tolerance for foreign exchange risk may be quite low. He may exact a heavy toll which exceeds the cost of hedging in the market. It is true that contract provisions can be added that allow for sharing the risk if the supplier is agreeable; however, exchange rate escalator clauses written into purchasing agreements by attorneys sometimes create even larger exposures than the foreign currency itself. Provisions dealing with foreign exchange must always be reviewed carefully in light of alternative hedging methods to see if they make sense.

There is another factor to be considered when transferring the exposure risk to the supplier. A few years ago, for example, a furniture manufacturer was contracting to buy an annual supply of lumber from a Canadian mill. During a corporate policy meeting, the company tried to get a handle on the resultant Canadian dollar exposure. Various suggestions were tossed about. The majority present began leaning toward denominating the contract in U.S. dollars, thereby avoiding foreign exchange exposure altogether. There were assurances that the supplier would agree; he was not in a position to object. At this point, however, one of the principals made a rather insightful observation:

> *"We know how to hedge," she said, "and we know how to do it right. (The supplier) has never hedged and doesn't understand it. If he tries, he may lose control of it, and get into deep financial straits. If he doesn't hedge, he may lose his shirt on the deal. Either way, we lose our supplier."*

Transferring the risk to the supplier in this case would only serve to exchange transactional exposure for less manageable operating exposure. The decision was made to contract in Canadian dollars, and to develop a hedge program toward that end.

Hedger to Customer

By far the most common method of transferring transactional exposure risk for U.S. companies, and by far the most risky, is to give it to the customer. The foreign exchange risk is transferred to the customer whenever catalogs and price sheets are sent overseas denominated in U.S. dollars. As far as foreign exchange problems go, *caveat emptor!* This method once worked. It still does, somewhat, but not as well as it used to. The international customer today doesn't have to buy American—or Japanese, German, or British for that matter. The bazaar is replete with competing products from every corner of the globe. Today there seems always to be a competitor in the wings who has no difficulty supplying just the right product at just the right price in just the right currency. Transferring risk to the customer accomplishes no more than trading visible (accounting) exposure for hidden (operating) exposure. Hidden long and short positions are easier to ignore, at least for a while, and thus always harder to get a handle on. Exporters ignore them at their peril. Accounting exposures disappear when sales are solely in U.S. dollars, but sometimes the markets tend to disappear right along behind them.

Parallel Markets

Hedging can only take place in parallel markets, defined as follows:

> *When an item is valued in one market at a price that correlates significantly with the price of a another item in another market, the two markets are considered to be parallel.*

The world is awash in parallel markets. Commodity traders are certainly familiar with them. They often deal in nothing else. Whenever two contracts are traded as a spread, the trade is—hopefully—in parallel markets. Spreads are used to pair up products such as soybeans and soybean oil, treasury bills and Eurodollars, gold and platinum, heating oil and crude oil, S&P 500 and Value line indices, *ad infinitum.* Then, of course, the futures market and the cash market in any single commodity can be paired. Also, calendar spreads can be seen as parallel markets (such as July wheat and December wheat). Another way to trade parallel markets is with options and futures, options and forwards, or futures and forwards.

Parallel markets require only one thing: the prices must move together (have a high correlation). They may move up and down in tandem, or mirror each other in an inverse relationship (such as bond prices and yields). Either way, there must be parallel price movement. The entire concept of hedging is based on such movement. Hedges only take place in two or more markets that parallel each other, with one "leg" in each. Considered in this manner, there is no fundamental difference between a hedge and a spread trade. With a hedge, however, one leg always constitutes the exposure.

Foreign currency hedges are not restricted to futures, forwards, options, and swaps. They can be constructed in different segments of the same cash market, as with our example of the Japanese auto maker who manufactures in the market place of its customer. In fact, parallel currency markets can consist of any two transactional activities that use the same currency. Assume, for example, that "Wear Forever," a British outdoor woolen wear manufacturer, sells to the Australian consumer market. In this operation, the company is long Australian dollars. Its cash flow is denominated in the local currency. It profits when the Australian dollar strengthens against its home currency; however, this long position is also an operating exposure, since a weaker Australian dollar can price the company's products—produced in pound sterling—out of the market. The company therefore hedges by forming a manufacturing venture with an Australian partner. Now it has a short Australian dollar position in the labor market, as well as in the local wool market. A weaker Australian dollar translates into lower production costs, allowing price margins to remain unchanged. The long position in the consumer market is offset by a short position in the parallel labor and materials markets. Of course, this is just another way of viewing risk transference to the market place.

Hedging means the offsetting of a given position by taking a position of equal size and opposite direction in a separate, but parallel, mar-

ket. *The effect of the offsetting position is to reduce or eliminate the effects of changes in the value of both positions.*

Figure 4-2: Parallel Markets

Parallel Market Transactions:
Hedging Accounting and Cash Flow Exposure

Market	Currency Position #1	Currency Position #2	Currency Position #3
Cash	Long	Short	
Forward	Long		Long
Option		Long	Short

Parallel Market Operations:
Hedging Cash Flow and Operating Exposure

Market	Currency Position #1	Currency Position #2	Currency Position #3
Consumer	Long	Short	Long
Labor	Short		Short
Raw Materials		Short	Short

Note: Hedges are produced by creating opposite currency exposures in parallel markets.

Basis and Correlation

"Basis" refers to the *difference between two prices.* Basis is central when spreads and hedges are entered. When someone talks about basis, it is taken for granted that he or she is referring to markets of related products, with prices that move in tandem (i.e., correlate) but the term does not *necessarily* imply a price correlation. It is meaningful, for example, to speak of the basis between Swiss francs and Deutsche marks, or Chicago wheat and Kansas City wheat, or the S&P 500 index and the Value Line index, but we can just as easily talk of the basis between Deutsche marks and Japanese yen, or gold and British pounds, or coffee and copper. The basis simply refers to the difference in price between any two things for which values can be assigned.

Figure 4-3: Charting Basis—1

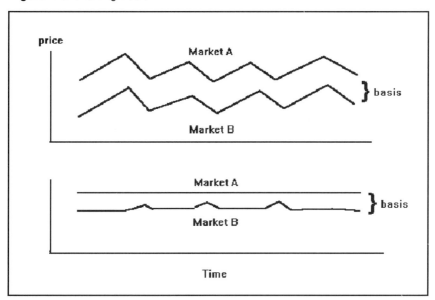

Figure 4-4: Charting Basis—2

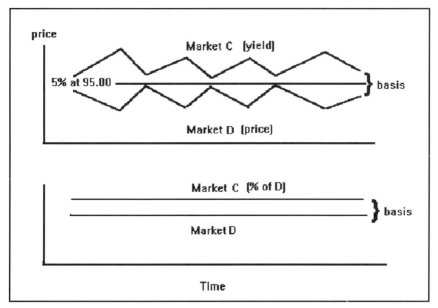

Figure 4-5: Charting Basis—3

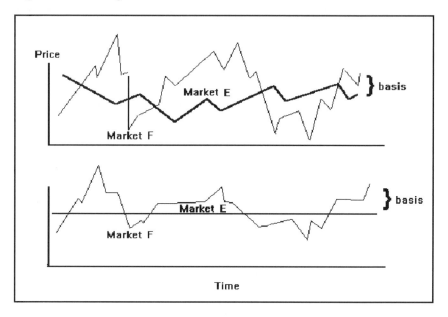

Correlation is measured as a coefficient between 0 and 1.00. A zero coefficient denotes random movements of the two prices relative to one another; 1.00 signifies prices moving in perfect lock step. Figures 4-3 through 4-5 show two price charts for each pair of markets. The upper chart of each pair shows individual price moves. The lower chart shows the price of one market held constant at zero value, and the price *difference* of the second market is plotted against this constant. This is known as a "basis chart." Basis is often referred to as a premium or a discount to the base line. Markets B and D, for example, are trading at a discount.

The basis between Markets A and B shows a high degree of correlation, with a coefficient well above 70%; therefore, these two markets are suitable for hedging purposes. Note that there can also be a high degree of *negative* correlation, such as with Markets C and D. Although mirror images of each other, the correlation is perfect, with a coefficient of 1.00. Markets C and D can provide nearly perfect hedges.

Reverse position hedges are used for negatively correlated markets. Assume, for example, that Market C represents the yield of a U.S. treasury bill in the cash market, and Market D represents the price of a futures contract for the same bill. They maintain a perfect negative correlation;

an uptick in yield is a down tick in price. If a hedger were *long* short-term interest rates, he would go *long* treasury bill futures. This, of course, is the opposite of a normal hedge, where a long exposure requires a short hedge position. In this case, however, the loss from a drop in interest rates is offset by a gain from the higher futures price.

Basis charts can be drawn for any two markets. If one were to measure the price relationship between feeder cattle and gold, Market E might be the value of 100 ozs. of gold over time, and Market F might be the price of feeder cattle over the same length of time. Most likely, the correlation coefficient would be zero!

Obviously, even in so-called parallel markets the price basis can be a wildly changing affair. One day it may be "narrow," meaning that the difference in prices is small. The next day the basis can be "wide," with prices far apart. If the markets do not relate to each other, the basis is often completely random. In fact, parallel markets are identified simply by analyzing the price basis between them. Where there is a correlation, there *may* be a parallel market. Basis is charted using historical price data, much as is done when working with exchange rates. What is most interesting is evidence of *predictability* in the correlation analyses. If there are two items with prices moving together in a highly predictable fashion over a significant period of time, they are not only *parallel* markets, but *hedgeable* parallel markets.

When are two markets highly correlated enough for hedging purposes? In general, if the correlation is .70 or higher, there is a good chance that the two markets can be used to construct a hedge; therefore, the definition of a hedge can be refined again as follows:

> *Hedging means offsetting a given position by taking an equal and opposite position in a separate but parallel market. The effect of the offsetting position is to reduce or eliminate the effects of changes in the value of both positions. Markets are sufficiently parallel if the correlation coefficient of the basis is 0.70 or higher.*

Convergence

There would be little likelihood of correlation if there were no mechanism for keeping the two markets parallel. A futures contract for copper, say, is prevented from trading away from the cash copper market by the fact that the contract can be converted into physical copper. It is this ability to exchange for physicals that maintained the price of gold at $35 an ounce during the Bretton Woods era. The same convertibility kept the value of the Mexican peso close to $0.35 for years. Without convertibility, there could be no arbitrage, and without the prospect of arbitrage there would be no price correlation. The most important aspect of convertibility, from a hedging standpoint, is price convergence. Price convergence occurs as a futures contract nears the delivery period. Carrying charges become minimal; therefore, the price of the futures contract nears the spot price of the underlying good. Convertability and convergence can be thought of as functions of each other. In fact, a general rule is:

> *Whenever there is a future point in time at which one market item can be converted easily and without significant cost into another market item, the two prices will converge at that time. The two markets will trade in parallel up until that time, with the basis maintaining a hedgeable correlation coefficient.*

Convergence by convertibility is critical in all futures trading, but it is especially significant with financial futures. This is because instruments such as treasury bond futures and Swiss franc futures not only assure convertibility, but also assure the *value of the conversion.* If a trader takes delivery of 125,000 Swiss francs, they will have the same value as the underlying "cash" Swiss franc, no more or less.

With foreign currency futures, there is no question about delivery, transportation, storage, or grade. You can be assured that the full value of the currency will be deposited in your account a few days after the last trading day. With value of conversion thus guaranteed, the cost and the risk of arbitraging mis-priced instruments is practically non-existent. As a result, the various exchange-traded derivatives of an underlying currency almost always have high correlation coefficients.

Parallel Currency Markets

An instrument with its value derived from the value of another instrument, commodity, or currency is classified as a "derivative." The value of a treasury bill futures contract depends on the value of the cash market treasury bill on which it is based; thus, the contract is a derivative of the cash bill. A British pound futures option is price-dependent on the spot and forward exchange rates between the dollar and the pound; therefore, the option is a derivative of the spot currency. Derivatives trade in markets that are parallel to the underlying cash market, whatever the item may be.

How does the concept of parallel market hedging apply to hedging methods such as operating strategies or financial adjustments? Say a company hedges by producing in the same country and in the same local currency as its overseas marketing subsidiary. Because both operations are transacted in the same market place (the spot market), one cannot be considered a derivative of the other. Is this, then, a parallel market hedge? We can indeed consider this to be a parallel market hedge, with one "leg" in each, by expanding the definition of parallel markets; therefore:

Any two transactions denominated in a single currency are parallel-market transactions if they offset exposure, but are single-market transactions if they cancel out exposure.

This completes the definition of hedging. Although somewhat contrived, it permits the financial advisor to speak to prospective users about parallel-market hedging, and include rather seamlessly every form of exposure management, be it market transactions, operating strategies, or financial adjustments.

CHAPTER 5

Foreign Currency Exposure

Years ago, the U.S. export market was an afterthought. The United States was the largest consumer market in the world. For decades, its rate of consumption climbed in a remarkable fashion. Demand was often difficult to satisfy even at full capacity. There were plenty of buyers to go around. Foreign markets were left to the foreigners.

Today the world is very different. The U.S. market, although still the primary consumer market of the world, is declining in relative importance because of accelerating purchasing power in the developing world. At the same time, ever-higher government expenditures at home reduce the quantity of dollars available for spending on consumer goods. Any company wishing to expand today, sooner or later must look offshore. This being the case, U.S. corporations are fast becoming aware that a great deal of time, expense, and effort is required to successfully market in a foreign country. Careful consideration must be given to the "marketing mix" and the four "Ps": product, place, price, and promotion. This raises a number of questions. Is this the right product? If not, how can it be modified to make it right? Is the product in the right place (suitable for the market, the culture, or the social climate)? What about price? Is it affordable? And finally, what is the best way to promote the product so that it competes successfully with similar products of other manufacturers?

Operating Exposure

Global competition has become so intense that every aspect of the marketing mix must be constantly reviewed. One particular area in which companies are winning or losing the battle for market share involves trade finance. Regardless of design, quality, and price, if the buyer can more easily afford a competitive product, chances are good that the competitor's product is what he will buy. The financial package offered to the buyer, therefore, becomes a bargaining chip. The best trade finance package for the *exporter*, of course, is cash in advance. That still is the requirement for many sales, primarily when transferring currency out of the buyer's country is seen as a major problem. To compete effectively, the exporter must usually offer more attractive terms. These are listed below, from the least to the most desirable, from the buyer's point of view:

1. *Cash in advance*;

2. *Letter of credit*, in which the buyer's bank assumes payment responsibility upon proof of shipment or receipt;

3. *Documentary collection*, in which the buyer's bank assumes payment responsibility upon the buyer's authorization;

4. *Open account*, in which the seller invoices the buyer directly, with payment terms agreed upon in advance;

5. *Local currency open account*, same as above with invoicing denominated in the buyer's currency.

Although many cross-border trade relations begin with cash in advance or letters of credit, the usual objective is to progress toward more "buyer friendly" methods of financing. This progression takes place as the counter-parties get to know each other, and as credit becomes established. Both the exporter and the importer benefit when the trade finance package becomes more attractive; the importer from a financial standpoint and the exporter from a marketing point of view.

Still, the majority of U.S. exporters refuse to offer the most attractive method of financing, which is invoicing in the buyer's currency on an open account basis. There are two reasons for this. First, the U.S. dollar has always been considered the accepted international invoicing currency. It is traditional to price in dollars. Secondly, the majority of U.S. companies do not know how to protect themselves from the foreign exchange risk introduced by local currency invoicing.

To avoid these obvious risks, the U.S. exporter invoices solely in U.S. dollars, and the U.S. importer sources only in U.S. dollars. By doing so, they both often unknowingly assume a foreign exchange *operating exposure*. This type of exposure is not immediately visible, as we learned in Chapter One. In fact, it is often referred to as a "hidden exposure."

There are different definitions of operating exposure, but they have common elements:

1. Operating exposure bears no necessary relationship to accounting exposure.

2. It is not necessarily associated with the country in which goods are sold or inputs sourced (such as the Chrysler Corporation's operation.)

3. It is not necessarily associated with the currency in which prices are quoted.

4. Profits or losses from operating exposure vary with changes in the real, rather than nominal, exchange rate.

5. Operating exposure is determined by the structure of the markets in which the company and its competitors source inputs and sell products.

The measurement of operating exposure must take into account both the nature of the company and its competition. (*Accounting exposure*, by contrast, is limited to measurements from the financial statements.) With few exceptions, operating exposure can be defined as the effect of foreign exchange on a company's competitive position, both at home and abroad.

Consider the trade finance package of a hypothetical U.S. manufacturer with a newly established distributorship in Mexico. As with all its customers, the manufacturer invoices in U.S. dollars. After a few shipments based on letters of credit, the director of finance feels confident enough to deal with its Mexican distributor on an open account basis. By now a well-cemented relationship exists between them; therefore, the director is surprised when the distributor abruptly closes out the line a few months later. Responding to urgent queries, the Mexican firm informs the manufacturer that it replaced the line with a competitive European line that is willing to invoice in Mexican pesos. "Remember," intones the distributor, "our function is to sell products, not to gamble in foreign currencies." The manufacturer lost market share due to operating exposure.

Managing Operating Exposure

One very effective way to deal with operating exposure is to convert it into another form of exposure. This is accomplished by denominating invoices in the currency of the buyer or, in the case of an importer, denominating purchase agreements in the currency of the supplier. This produces accounting or cash flow exposures which the company must then contend with, but there are methods for handling these.

Operating exposure can also be managed by employing one or more operating strategies. Most of these involve an actual change in the method of doing business. They are meant to be permanent fixes, and are never entered into lightly. Usually they are authorized at the level of the board of directors, and virtually never below the level of senior management. The following strategies are the ones most often considered:

1. *Retrenchment*—Perhaps the most effective way to avoid risk of exposure is not to hedge it, but to eliminate it. The strategy is simple: do not remain involved in the market of the particular currency creating the exposure. The question of whether the market potential really is worth the attendant exposure is always a legitimate one. If the company is already exposed in a foreign market, has the situation changed enough to warrant a second look at it? There are, of course, other considerations at least as important when deciding whether to remain in a particular country. A change in the political or social climate may be decisive. Pulling out of markets is done regularly for any number of reasons. Reducing currency exposure is one of them.

2. *Siting*—Another method of hedging foreign exchange exposure involves siting of manufacturing facilities. If a new foreign market looks promising, with potential for significant penetration, can some of the production be shifted to that country either with new construction or by buying an existing facility? The idea here is to match the currency of revenue with the currency in which goods and inventory are priced.

3. *Changing the Mix*—Exposures might be reduced or offset by changing the mix of marketing and production. This strategy is especially appropriate for an acquisition-minded growing company; for example, a company that produces in the United States and markets in Germany may decide to acquire a German firm that produces a complementary line of products. These products would then be imported to the U.S. market. In this way, long exposures resulting from Deutsche mark revenues and U.S. dollar costs are offset by short exposures resulting from U.S. dollar revenues and Deutsche mark costs.

4. *Product Modification*—Modification of the product line can help reduce the exposure from foreign currency. There may be a product line that is very sensitive to price change, such as a low-cost consumer item with little or no differentiation. The item may be

priced out of a foreign market because it is competing against a weaker-currency based product. Perhaps the item can be retargeted and promoted to a different market segment, one that is less price sensitive. Perhaps it can be modified to differentiate it from the competition, making it less sensitive to price.

5. *Sourcing Flexibility*—Siting of manufacturing facilities for the purpose of reducing exposure can be done on a less grandiose scale. So-called "screwdriver" facilities, used to assemble components at a minimal skill level, sometimes are comprised of nothing more than metal structures on dirt floors lined with benches. Such facilities are located in countries where labor is relatively cheap. They are relatively inexpensive to start up, shut down, and move around, compared to full-scale manufacturing units. There may be several such facilities sited, with production shifted among them based on currency strengths and weaknesses. This method is used to reduce exposure, and also to take advantage of weaker currencies as they occur, thereby obtaining a competitive edge in other markets.

Accounting Exposure

When a company invoices or purchases in a foreign currency, it takes on a different set of problems. It confronts an accounting exposure. This is the risk of foreign currency change as it relates to the financial statements. Several other terms are sometimes used to define this type of risk. For example, we often hear of *balance sheet* exposure, *transactional* exposure, *translation* exposure, *consolidated* exposure, etc.

Because it shows up on the financial statements, accounting exposure is quite visible. This visibility makes it the most troublesome form of risk for many financial officers. Therefore, most of your consulting efforts will be directed toward managing these accounting exposures. After all, stockholders and creditors scrutinize the company's financial statements more rigorously than they do its distributors' and competitors'! The balance sheet is often produced just four times each year, and the values reported are those that exist on each of those four particular days. They may be quite different from the values the day before or the day after the reporting date. The exposed currency position, then, is simply a snapshot. It is a static view, and not very useful in projecting the future impact the exposure will have on the company. For this reason, exposure management that concentrates solely on the balance sheet may bring about more pervasive foreign exchange risk.

Look at the financial statements in Figures 5-1 and 5-2 from a hypothetical company, Rocker Inc.

A multinational, it has operations spanning a number of countries. One operation is an office furniture manufacturing unit, headquartered in the United States. This unit constructs finished office partitions to sell in various overseas markets. The wood used in construction is purchased from a Canadian supplier.

Figure 5-1: Rocker, Incorporated

Consolidated Balance Sheet
(in millions)

Assets		Liabilities and Shareowners' Equity	
Current Assets		*Current Liability*	
Cash and short term investments	213	Accounts payable	686
Receivables, net	314	Notes Payable	493
Prepaid expenses & other current assets	136	Accrued Liabilities	650
Deferred income tax benefit	67	Other Current Liabilities	236
Inventories	452	**Total Current Liabilities**	**2,065**
Total Current Assets	**1,182**		
		Long Term Debt	1,115
Property, Building and Equipment		Deferred Income Taxes	388
Property	937	Other Liabilities	374
Buildings	1,363		
Equipment	3,052	**Shareholders' Equity**	
Construction in Process	166	Preferred Stock	234
Total Property, Bldgs & Equip at cost	5,518	Common Stock	788
Less Accumulated Depreciation	-1,876	Retained Earnings	1,434
Total net property, Bldgs & Equip	**3,642**	Less Common Stock in Treasury	-394
Other non-current assets	**189**	Cumulative Foreign Currency Adj.	-18
		Total Shareholders' Equity	**2,044**
Other Assets			
Intangible Assets	65		
Investments in affiliates			
(foreign & domestic)	629		
Miscellaneous Assets	289		
Total Other Assets	**983**	**Total Liabilities and**	
Total Assets	**5,996**	**Shareholders' Equity**	**5,996**

Figure 5-2: Rocker Incorporated

Statement of Consolidated Income (in millions of U.S. dollars. Except per Share Data)	Fiscal Years Ended	
	12/31/94	12/31/93
Sales	12,595	10,313
Gain/Loss on Currency Translation	232	-206
Net Sales	**12,363**	**10,707**
Costs and Expenses		
Cost of Goods Sold	7,808	5,672
Selling, Administrative & General Costs	3,230	3,106
Interest Expense	463	403
Pension Expense	80	69
Depreciation	113	103
Total Costs and Expenses	**11,694**	**9,353**
Income from Continuing Operations Before Taxes	669	754
Income Taxes (U.S. & Foreign)	122	176
Income from Continuing Operations	**547**	**578**
Income per share—Continuing Operations	$8.29	$8.76
Discontinued Operations After Taxes	34	
Net Income	**581**	**578**
Net Income per share	$8.81	$8.76
Average Number of Common Shares	66	66

The values in parentheses in Figure 5-3 represent the U.S. dollar value of the Canadian dollar assets and liabilities from this operation. Because the balance sheet consolidates the figures of all operations, these values are only a fraction of the total. Remember that these are static values, and apply only on the date that the balance sheet is prepared.

Figure 5-3: U.S. Dollar Value of the Canadian Dollar Assets and Liabilities

	Worldwide Operations (U.S. $ in millions)	Portion allotted to Canadian Oper. (U.S. $ in millions)
Assets:		
Current Assets		
Cash and short term investments	213	(7)
Receivables (net)	314	(79)
Inventories	452	(23)
Total		(109)
Property, Building and Equipment		
Construction in Process	166	(12)
Total		(12)
Liabilities and Shareowners' Equity		
Current Liability		
Accounts payable	686	(65)
Notes Payable	493	(14)
Total		(79)

    The Canadian dollar exposure tells us something about the nature of the operation. The company pays the Canadian mill in the mill's local currency, thereby incurring Canadian dollar payables. Some lumber is inventoried at the mill or in box cars on a siding, which shows up in the inventory values. The company also sells the finished partitions in Canada through distributors, and has outstanding receivables from these sales. Apparently, the company is in the process of building a mill in Canada to supply the Canadian market better, which accounts for the property under construction and the notes payable to a Canadian bank to help finance it.

    The "bottom line" exposure is the sum of the U.S. dollar value of foreign currency-denominated assets less the U.S. dollar value of foreign currency-denominated liabilities. Notice that the company has a net short-term Canadian dollar asset exposure worth US$30 million ($109 million - $79 million). It has an additional long-term asset exposure worth US$12 million.

    It is important to recognize that each of these book entries comprises a *foreign currency transaction*. In other words, the company is transacting—thereby acquiring assets and incurring liabilities—in a currency other than its home currency. The currency used in the normal course of business and the one in which it denominates its financial reports is, of course, the U.S. dollar, which is referred to as the *functional currency* of the company. Any currency other than the functional currency is called a *nonfunctional currency.*

Transactional Exposure

Accounting exposure resulting from nonfunctional currency transactions of a parent company is called transactional exposure. In small- to medium-sized companies, (particularly those relatively new to exporting or importing), that have no foreign subsidiaries and centralize all financial transactions in one department, transactional exposure is the only form of accounting exposure incurred.

Different types of transactional exposure are treated in different ways for accounting and tax purposes. Accepted practices are those put forth in statements issued by the Financial Accounting Standards Board, or FASB. The FASB Statement 52 deals specifically with foreign currency exposure. According to FASB 52, the current value of the foreign currency must be used to prepare financial reports. Assets and liabilities must be "marked to the market." Any gains or losses incurred from changes in exchange rates between the time the transaction occurred and the time the balance sheet is prepared must be reported as a separate line item on the income statement. This item is designated "Gain/Loss on Currency Translation" in the income statement above.

This procedure is troublesome to financial managers because the foreign exchange gain or loss must be included in the income statement; therefore, it directly affects earnings and profitability, with consequent tax implications. Such high visibility accounts for the sometimes herculean efforts that some companies make to hedge or reduce transactional exposure. Rocker Inc's income statement shows a foreign currency loss of $232 million dollars, a loss which reflects depreciating-currency assets, appreciating-currency liabilities, or both. Such loss can certainly have a major impact on profitability for a multinational with a large percentage of its business in nonfunctional currencies.

Translation Exposure

Let's assume that the objective of Rocker Inc.'s construction program in Canada is to build a furniture production facility which will be a wholly owned subsidiary. The production facility will operate as an autonomous unit. It will have its own executive management team, including a treasury department to handle the finances. The balance sheet and the income statement of the unit will be prepared in Canadian dollars, then submitted to Rocker Inc. for inclusion in the consolidated financial statement.

The act of translating the figures of the Canadian subsidiary into U.S. dollars for consolidation introduces another form of accounting exposure. This is called translation exposure. Like transactional exposure, the assets and liabilities of the subsidiary must be marked to the market. Again, the resulting gains and losses occurring from one reporting period to another must be broken out and reported in compliance with FASB 52; however, in this case, the value derived concerns exchange rate fluctuations of a *functional* currency, the one used for everyday business. The Canadian dollar, after all, is the currency used in the normal course of business by the subsidiary booking the assets and liabilities.

This is an important distinction, because functional currency translation results are reported differently from nonfunctional currency transactional gains and losses. In this case, the gain or loss does not flow through to the income statement, and so it does not have profitability or tax implications. Instead, it is relegated to the shareholders' equity section of the balance sheet as a foreign-currency adjustment. This is viewed by the accounting industry as a rather "out of the way" place. There appears to be a tacit understanding that adjustments to equity need not be scrutinized to the same degree as the income statement. In any event, translation exposure is less onerous than transactional exposure, at least in the near term. The items in Figure 5-4 from Rocker Inc.'s balance sheet show where translation exposure appears, and how it is reported.

Figure 5-4: Detail from Rocker, Inc. Balance Sheet

Other Assets:	
Investments in Affiliates (Foreign and domestic)	629
Shareholders' Equity:	
Cumulative Foreign Currency Adj. -18	

Managing Transactional Exposure (Short-Term)

Transactional exposure, more than any other kind, is most adaptable to management by financial hedging. This is because of the "like characteristics" of the exposure and the hedging vehicles. Assets and liabilities are contractual in nature; they are monetized, and have a known value. They often have a known duration. Short-term financial contracts have the same characteristics. This includes futures, forward contracts, and options. It also includes short-term borrowings.

An example of short-term borrowing can easily demonstrate the basic principal that underlies all hedging techniques. This is the application of equal and opposite positions (see Chapter Four). Here, borrowing creates an equal and opposite position in the financial arena to match an existing one in the cash market. Figure 5-5 illustrates an existing cash market (long) position in the form of a C$1,000,000 receivable. This is offset with an opposite (short) position in the financial market by borrowing C$1,000,000. Then, six months later when the receivable is collected, the bank loan is paid off with the proceeds. The change in foreign exchange rates has no effect on the original U.S. dollar value of the receivable.

Figure 5-5: Hedging a Short-Term Receivable

Existing Exposure	Create Offset Exposure
C$1,000,000 Receivable in 6 months	
C$ price: $0.71	1. Borrow C$1,000,000 from the bank
	2. Swap the C$ back to the bank for US $ (this constitutes the receivable)
six months later	
Collect C$1,000,000 C$ price: $0.70	3. Use the proceeds to repay the C$1,000,000
Loss $10,000	Gain $10,000

Figure 5-6 shows the reverse of this hedge. Here, there is an existing payable, or short position. A cash deposit of the same amount creates an offsetting long financial position. The principle of hedges of equal size and opposite direction applies regardless of the hedging vehicle used.

Figure 5-6: Hedging a Short-Term Payable

Existing Exposure	Create Offset Exposure
C$1,000,000 Payable in 6 months	
C$ price: $0.71	1. Buy C$1,000,000 spot from a bank
	2. Hold in the account
six months later	
Payment due C$ price : $0.70	3. Transfer C$ to payee the C$1,000,000
Gain$10,000	Loss $10,000

The list in Figure 5-7 contains alternative hedging vehicles that can be used in lieu of bank borrowings or cash deposits. Notice that the transaction details change in each case, but the underlying principle remains exactly the same.

The examples in Figures 5-8 and 5-9 (p. 102) illustrate that the effects of foreign exchange fluctuations are canceled out by the gains and losses incurred during the time the hedge is in place.

A cursory look at these examples may elicit a few protests if you use them with a corporate client. You can probably expect the following reaction:

"Wait a minute. I thought these futures hedges were the same as non-leveraged bank transactions, which cancel out foreign exchange rate changes. In these examples, the gains and losses are totally different."

The reason is that interest rates are factored in, but not shown. When protecting a receivable by borrowing Canadian dollars and then swapping them for U.S. dollars, a Canadian dollar interest rate cost is incurred and U.S. dollar interest rate earnings accrue (assuming that the U.S. dollars are deposited in an interest-bearing account until the receivable is collected). The difference between the interest paid and the interest collected during six months should just about equal the difference between the gain and the loss realized on the futures hedge.

Figure 5-7: Various Long- and Short-Hedge Positions

Have acquired long receivable—therefore hedge with one of the following positions:

Short position:	*from:*	*Characteristics:*
bank debt	bank	no leverage
short forward contract	bank	leverage: credit line
short futures contract	broker	leverage: margin account
Put option	broker/ dealer	no leverage (loss limited to premium)

Have acquired short payable—therefore hedge with one of the following positions:

Long Position	*from:*	*Characteristics:*
Cash deposit	bank	no leverage
Long forward contract	bank	leverage: credit line
Long futures contract	broker	leverage: margin account
Call option	broker/ dealer	no leverage (loss limited to premium)

Figure 5-8: Foreign Exchange Fluctuations

cash	futures
March 1st...	
Receivable **1,000,000 at .7128**	**Sell (go short)** **10 CS September Contracts** **at .7073**
6 months later...	
Receive **1,000,000 C$ at .7010**	**Buy back (go long)** **10 C$ September Contracts** **at .6998**
Loss - $11,800	**Gain - $7,500**

Figure 5-9: Foreign Exchange Fluctuations

cash	futures
March 1st...	
Payable **1,000,000 at .7128**	**Buy back (go long)** **10 CS September Contracts** **at .7073**
6 months later...	
Pay **1,000,000 C$ at .7010**	**Sell (go short)** **10 C$ September Contracts** **at .6998**
Gain - $11,800	**Loss - $7,500**

In the above example of the bank transaction used to hedge a payable, the hedger buys Canadian dollars and holds them until the payable becomes due. In this case, a purchase of C$1,000,000 requires $700,000, which he borrows for the purpose. This implies an interest rate cost, as well as an interest rate earning on the currency held. Again, the difference between the two rates of interest for six months will account for most of the difference between the cash market gain and the futures loss (see Chapter Three).

Managing Transactional Exposure (Long-Term)

Futures, forward contracts, and options are useful out to about a year. Beyond that, the market gets very thin and pricing becomes more of an art form than a math problem. There are instruments called long-term forward contracts that go out to five years or more. They are not very popular because they are very illiquid and the pricing is so imprecise. There is also a way to hedge a multi-year exposure by continuously rolling over six-month forward or futures contracts, but this is not a perfect solution, either. The forward rates are always changing because of changes in the interest rate differentials, which are left unhedged. The discussion of cash flow exposure below will give further insight into long-term transactional hedging.

Hedge Accounting and FASB 52

"Deferred accounting" of hedge transactions means that hedge gains and losses are not taxed until the corresponding loss or gain from the exposure is realized. Then, the offsetting balances become non-taxable events; only the net balance is taxable (as a debit or a credit, depending on whether the balance is a loss or a gain). It is important to adhere to the accepted accounting standards regarding hedge definitions in order to take advantage of deferred accounting practices. For this reason, you must know whether your client is using FASB 52 or some other standard. The arena of hedge accounting is a dynamic one, and you should make a point of knowing the latest interpretations and revisions pertaining to the subject.

Hedging activity centers around transaction exposure, since it is most visible. FASB 52 currently allows more flexibility in the construction of translation hedges than was once the case. Previously, hedge vehicle selection was restricted to forward contracts, which had to be in the same currency that created the exposure. Substitute currencies that trade in more-liquid markets were disallowed. This is no longer the case; proxy hedging with other currencies is now permitted. (Deutsche marks can be used to hedge Dutch guilder exposures, for example.) Futures, swaps, and options are now allowed; however, the criterion of the particular exposures that can be hedged remains unchanged; i.e., contractual agreements of certain value in a foreign currency. Thus, hedge accounting practices are limited to transactional or translation exposure. According to FASB 52, to be considered a hedge, a transaction must:

- offset an identifiable foreign currency commitment;
- be designated as, and effective as, a hedge;
- must be a firm commitment in its own right (a matter of fact, not form).

Managing Translation Exposure

As we discussed, the difference between translation exposure and transactional exposure has to do with whether or not the company is transacting in a functional or nonfunctional currency. A foreign subsidiary that conducts business in the local currency produces no exposure until the financial reports are translated into the currency of the parent company. Before the advent of FASB 52, questions arose concerning the proper value to use in the translation. Should the historical or current exchange rate be applied? The historical rate refers to the one in effect when the exposure was initially contracted. Now, all translations are marked to the current market value, with value differences between one reporting period and the next entered as a special item in the shareholder's equity section of the balance sheet.

Certainly, short-term instruments like futures and forwards are not suitable for locking in the value of long-term assets such as plant, equipment, and other capital investments, or the long-term debt incurred by the company to pay for them. Long-term exposures are managed most effectively by infusing capital into the operation in the form of local bank borrowings in the foreign currency to create short positions, or by investing local currency in the country of the operation to hedge long-term liabilities. Long-term borrowing as a hedge is described more fully below.

A special situation exists in countries with highly inflationary economies, which, according to FASB 52, are defined as those with a three year inflation rate of approximately 100% or more. The local currency of a highly inflationary economy is considered nonfunctional, according to FASB 52, and currency exposure should be treated as transactional exposure. This makes sense because a rapidly depreciating currency can hardly fulfill the role of a reporting standard unit of measure in any event.

Cash Flow Exposure

Figure 5-10 diagrams the cash flows of a multinational corporation. The parent corporation is located in the United States, so its functional currency is the U.S. dollar. It has several manufacturing facilities abroad. Product is shipped from manufacturing to marketing subsidiaries, which are located in their region. These are regions such as Europe, Southeast Asia, and Latin America. The marketing subsidiaries sell to independent distributors both within their country and in the surrounding nations. The parent corporation and the manufacturing units invoice and remit to each other in U.S. dollars.

Figure 5-10: Multinational Currency Flows

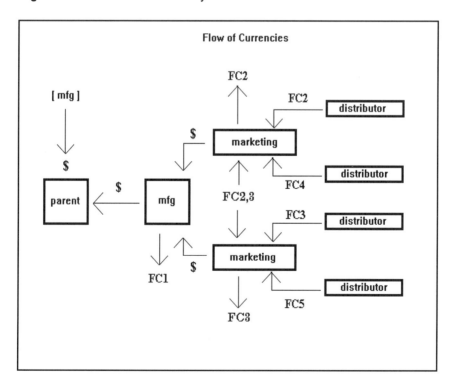

The diagram in Figure 5-10 illustrates the following cash flows:

- The manufacturing unit submits U.S. dollar-denominated invoices to the marketing subsidiaries and transfers dollar-denominated receivables to the parent corporation. Otherwise, it functions in its local currency (FC1) regarding operating expenses, taxes, etc.

- Marketing units within each region remit the transfer price in dollars to manufacturing, and pay operating expenses in their local currencies (FC2 and FC3).

- The marketing units invoice their domestic distributors in the local currency, but invoice foreign distributors in the distributor's currency (FC2, 3, 4 or 5).

- In addition, all units buy and sell among themselves, each invoicing in its local currency. As shown, various cash flows are denominated in at least six currencies.

Whereas accounting exposure looks backward and provides "snap shots" of the effect of exchange rate fluctuations as of a specific date, cash flow exposure looks at exposure in motion. It is concerned with ongoing changes, not just the divergence from one accounting period to the next. Measurement of cash flow exposure not only compares current results with past performance, but also anticipates future revenue streams, future sales, projected costs, and other budget items. If we think of accounting exposure as static, cash flow exposure is dynamic. The impact that cash flow exposure can have on profitability is staggering. One can point to RJR Nabisco, for example, with revenues worth more than one billion dollars annually from sales to more than 160 countries, all denominated in local currencies. With exposures in exchange rates between Deutsche marks, Italian lira, French francs, and Japanese yen, a reshuffling of the European Monetary System can translate into millions of dollars gained or lost overnight. Folding the European currencies into a single currency will create even more havoc in exchange rate adjustment.

Remember that accounting and cash flow exposures are just different ways of looking at foreign currency risk. Because foreign currency inflows and outflows generate new mismatches in assets and liabilities, today's cash flow exposure is tomorrow's accounting exposure. Cash flow exposure results in an *operating variance* between reporting periods, such as year to year. In other words, operating income increases and decreases in direct response to currency rate changes. This is not the focus of accounting exposure, which only affects translation adjustments once every three months. The difference between cash flow exposure and accounting exposure depends mainly on *when* the translation occurs.

Consider the four scenarios, each showing a relationship between operating variance and translation adjustment.[1] These relationships are depicted in Figure 5-11. In each case, the reporting period begins with a current FC/HC rate of 1.00.

Figure 5-11: Relationship Between Operating Variance and Translation
          Adjustment

	Case #1	Case #2	Case #3	Case#4
Total Revenues in FC	10,000	10,000	10,000	10,000
HC equivalent on first date of reporting period	10,000	10,000	10,000	10,000
Average HC equivalent throughout reporting period	10,000	10,000	9,000	9,500
HC Equivalent on balance sheet date	10,000	9,000	9,000	9,000
Operating variance	0	0	(1,000)	(500)
Transactional adjustment	0	(1,000)	0	(500)
Total impact on profitability	0	(1,000)	(1,000)	(1,000)

- Case # 1—FC remains stable. FC10,000 in revenue is derived from sales over a one-year period. This revenue is exposed to changes in the FC/HC exchange rate. In this case, there is no exchange rate change during the year and no impact on the financial statements.

- Case # 2—FC devalues on the balance sheet date. The FC10,000 is recorded as an asset of HC 10,000 until the balance sheet date. A devaluation on that date results in a translation adjustment of (HC1,000). The loss is a result of accounting exposure.

- Case # 3—FC devalues on the date revenue begins. On that date, revenues are recorded at an exchange rate of HC0.9. The rate does not change during the period, and no translation adjustment is recorded; however, there is an operating variance of (HC1,000) from the previous period. The decreased profits are attributable to cash flow exposure.

- Case # 4—FC devalues gradually over the reporting period. In this case, revenues continue to be recorded at ever lower HC values. The portion of devaluation before each revenue amount is recorded shows up as an operating adjustment. Once the revenues and expenses are booked, further devaluation is identified as a translation loss and adjusted as such. The losses are a result of both accounting and cash flow exposures.

Actually, all four cases have the same exposure and the same risk. Because cash flow exposure measures variances in operating income, it surfaces when making comparisons between the financial performance for two periods. Accounting exposure is found on the balance sheet and income statement, while cash flow exposure is found primarily on the statement of consolidated income when foreign operation performance for the current year is measured against the previous year, or it may appear in the letter to shareholders, where financial results are analyzed against past performance and future expectations.

Because cash flow exposure results in operating variances, it is often isolated by a method known as *variance analysis.* This type of analysis is conducted by picking apart the figures to identify the causes of the various changes between current and previous periods. After the changes are analyzed, they can be properly accounted for, with gains and losses due to exchange rate changes recognized either as translation adjustments or as operating variances. Variances due to factors other than foreign exchange-changes in management policies, for example-are all given their separate values.

Management of Cash Flow Exposure

Management of cash flow exposure is still being developed. Unlike balance sheet hedging, with which existing transactions are protected, hedging in currency markets to offset an anticipated operating variance falls outside the realm of standardized hedge accounting practices. Rather than sorting out assets and liabilities to find a net exposure, anticipatory models must be set up, and projections and forecasts play a much more important role. Put-'em-on-and-forget-'em hedges can work for accounting exposures, where the risk is contractual and unchanging; however, they are deadly for protecting cash flow. This type of exposure requires continual hands-on management as the actual figures and revised projections flow in. If the projection is wrong and the anticipated amount of mismatched currency does not equal the amount of the hedge, a foreign currency manager can suddenly find himself a currency speculator. This is why the FASB is reluctant to establish accounting standards for cash flow exposure.

In Chapter One, we considered three types of hedges: *operating strategies, transactional hedging,* and *financial adjustments.* We've found the first to be the most suitable for operating exposure. Accounting exposure can be managed quite well with the second type, transactional hedging. The third type, financial adjustments, defines methods that lie half way between the first two. Financial adjustments are not as time consuming, as expensive, nor as permanent as the operating strategies listed above. Although they are more flexible than operating strategies, they are not as flexible as transactional hedges. Financial adjustments as hedging techniques seem well suited for cash flow exposure.

We've listed below the various adjustments and transactions usually considered for the management of cash flow exposure. Remember that they are not permanent solutions and should not be considered as such. Flexibility is the key to cash flow exposures, and the degree of flexibility offered by each method is of paramount concern in the selection process.

- *Home-Currency Invoicing*—One common financial adjustment is to revert from foreign currency to home currency invoicing. The company simply prices everything in the home currency, such as the U.S. dollar. This method is most effective when the product line is unique and not price driven. Pharmaceuticals and other high tech items are good examples. Home currency invoicing should be continuously monitored because it invites competition from countries with weaker currencies. Also, if price sensitivity increases, the market itself may simply disappear.

- *Strong-Currency Invoicing*—There may be instances when a choice of invoicing currency is available, but the home currency is not among the options. Then, the best hedge is to invoice in the strongest currency, where there is a better chance for gain. For example, if invoicing can be denominated either in ECUs or in Deutsche marks and the Deutsche mark is the strongest currency in the ECU composite, then Deutsche marks should be the invoice currency.

- *Home-Currency Sourcing*—Here, inventories of components are bought and paid for in the home currency wherever possible. The purchasing department of a U.S. corporation favors the foreign vendors who agree to invoice in U.S. dollars. This assumes that the finished product is to be sold in the home currency. Again, it is a way of transferring the risk to a different party. It works as long as the vendors agree to accept the risk. There are caveats. Marginally profitable vendors may be unable to afford the additional burden, and vendors who do accept the risk often add the potential cost to their price quotes.

- *Same-Currency Sourcing*—An alternative is to find suppliers in the same country that is producing the revenue exposure. Purchasing from those sources in the local currency will help hedge the exposure. This is similar to sourcing methods described above as an operation strategy, but on a shorter-term contract basis.

- *Long-Term Fixed-Rate Borrowing*—This is perhaps the most common method used to hedge long-term translation exposures; for example, a firm that constructs a plant or distribution facility abroad finances the construction and operation in local currency from a local bank.

    The ensuing revenue is then offset by the payment of principal and interest over a number of years. This hedges exposure to nominal exchange rate changes. What remains is risk of change in the real rate of exchange because fixed-interest-rate loans do not compensate for changes in inflation. Because the greater exposure of fixed assets, over time, is to the real rate of exchange, this method affords only a partial hedge solution.

    Long-term foreign currency borrowing can be used to hedge cash flow exposure as well. The proceeds from the loan must be converted into the home currency to reduce the exposure. Repayment is made by reconverting the currency at higher or lower rates, offsetting risk to future foreign currency revenue. Borrowing funds from foreign banks to take out of the country in the form of another currency can involve some intricate maneuvering around foreign exchange regulations. Two strategies used are to pay out the proceeds as dividends, and to use them for paying off existing loans to the parent company.

- *Leading and Lagging*—This approach is quite suitable in organizations that have consolidated their various foreign currency exposures. Subsidiaries in strong-currency countries are subject to fast turn around when they submit invoices for payment; however, they are given surplus time to pay off their internal debts. Subsidiaries in weak-currency countries receive the opposite treatment; payment is withheld for 30, 60, or 90 days after they submit the invoice, but when they buy internally, prepayment or cash on delivery is required.

This method, along with the others that differentiate between strong-currency countries and weak-currency countries, are really just ways of trading the market. The position is based on the prospect that strong currencies will continue to strengthen, and weak currencies will continue to weaken. That may or may not happen. "Leading and lagging" is a sensible approach; however, when working with currencies that are rapidly changing in value. This adjustment to scheduling is appropriate with either a single foreign operation or for handling the numerous currencies involved in certain multinational operations. It can be used in external cash management, as well as internal transfers. After allowing for credit considerations, it makes sense to pay certain vendors more quickly than others and to bill certain customers more quickly than others.

Forward Roll-over

Fixed-rate borrowing from a local bank in a foreign country is a financial adjustment hedge. Such borrowings can also be accomplished by using the futures exchanges or the interbank, rather than the local bank. You recall that a *forward exchange swap* is initiated by simultaneously taking two forward positions (or a spot and a forward position) one long, the other short. Essentially, this is equivalent to borrowing the foreign currency for a certain amount of time at a fixed rate of interest. Foreign currency proceeds are received on the value date of the long position and paid back on the value date of the short position. The implied interest cost is calculated as the difference between the two rates.

If a hedger transacts a forward exchange swap and does not wish to pay back the currency to fulfill the short position, he doesn't have to. Instead, he simply takes a new long position to offset the existing short, and establishes a new short position for a value date even more distant. He makes these transactions simultaneously. This is called a *roll-over.* By this technique, a forward position can be maintained indefinitely through a continuous series of roll-overs. The only practical difference between rolling over forward contracts and a traditional long-term fixed-rate loan is the interest rate adjustment. The interest rate is subject to change each time the forward is rolled over because each newly established short forward will reflect the rate of interest in effect when the position is entered.

If you use futures contracts, you can simulate the forward roll over with a series of calendar spreads in currency futures or in options. As one position expires, simply close it out and open another position farther out. Again, you can maintain this proxy position for foreign currency borrowing as long as necessary.

The Anatomy of a Currency Swap

Another way to make a financial adjustment is through currency swaps, simulating long-term bank borrowing. A currency swap, and the closely related interest rate swap, are based on the concept of the foreign exchange swap described on page 33. Currency swaps, however, are constructed in a much different manner. These complex derivatives can be demystified by taking a step-by-step view. Let's start by reviewing examples of spot and forward transactions.

Assume the following:

FC / HC	=	2.00 (spot)
FC / HC	=	1.90 (1-year forward)
Eurorate for HC	=	10% per annum
Eurorate for FC	=	5% per annum
(transaction costs are ignored)		

Company 'H' requires 2,000,000 units of foreign currency (*FC*) to loan to its foreign subsidiary for capital improvements. It needs the FC 2,000,000 immediately, so it calls its bank with which it has established a line of credit for foreign exchange, and initiates a spot transaction (see Figure 5-12).

Figure 5-12: Spot Transaction

The company knows that it will be paid back by its subsidiary after one year has elapsed; therefore, it has an exposure for twelve months. The company decides to hedge this exposure by selling FC one-year forward (see Figure 5-13).

Figure 5-13: One-Year Forward Contract

These transactions may be combined into one, constituting a foreign exchange swap between Company 'H' and the bank (see Figure 5-14).

Figure 5-14: Foreign Exchange Swap

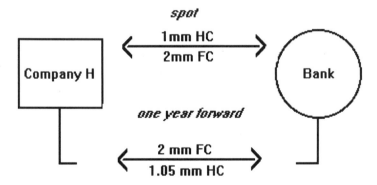

For this transaction, Company H deals directly with its bank, which is the usual method of accessing the interbank at a retail level. The bank, however, seeks to offset its exchange transactions with other dealers or other clients. Consider the same transaction with two counterparties, neither being the bank. Here the bank becomes an intermediary, "passing through" the transaction by taking the opposite side of the bid/offer spread with each counterparty. For a counterparty, assume that Company 'F' is located in the FC country. Its requirements mirror those of Company H: it needs HC 1,000,000 for one year, after which it will pay back the funds. Company H and Company F are not aware of each other. As far as each is concerned, it is dealing only with the bank (see Figure 5-15).

Figure 5-15: Foreign Exchange Swap

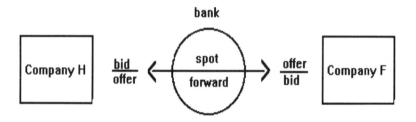

Although futures and forward contracts work well for managing individual accounting exposures with a year or less duration, they are less effective for the uncertain and variable exposures of cash flow, or for durations of more than a year. The currency swap market evolved to answer these specific needs. The swap consists of a written contract or agreement between two counterparties with opposite exposures. The bank may act as a match maker, finding a counterparty and facilitating the agreement, or it may act as a swap dealer and take the role of one of the counterparties. Assume the first relationship, in which case Company H and Company F are brought into direct contact with each other.

At this point, the companies are no longer dealing with a simple verbal foreign exchange swap. The transaction is now a currency swap, transacted in the form of a written agreement. The differences involve (1) duration (currency swaps typically are for one to ten years or more), and (2) customized terms and payment schedules (currency swaps are contracted with terms and considerations that do not necessarily comply with forward contract terms).

One feature of the swap is the ability to take advantage of creditworthiness. More than an exchange of currency is involved here. The elements of lending and borrowing are also in evidence. For this example, say that Company 'H' does not have strong lender relations in country FC and would have to pay a premium to borrow FC from a foreign bank. In its own country, however, it has a strong credit rating, allowing it to borrow at favorable rates. The reverse situation applies to Company 'F.' The swap allows each to take advantage of the other's borrowing power.

Now, view the above transaction as a one-year currency swap. Again, the bank only facilitates the swap as an intermediary. The contract terms are the same as for a regular spot/forward swap, but are now in written contract form binding on both counterparties. The bank introduces the parties, brokers the deal, then drops out of the picture (see Figure 5-16).

Figure 5-16: Currency Swap

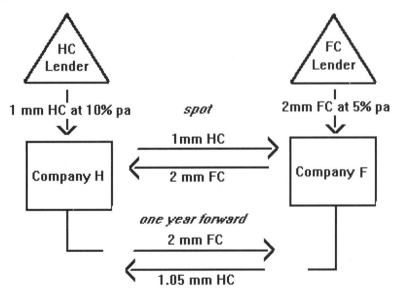

Finally, extend the transaction from one year to five years. The swap rate, defined as the difference in value between the spot and forward rates, no longer can be easily calculated. After one year, the interest rate picture becomes murky, the longer the yield curve, the more subject to unpredictable change. The type of exposure changes. This area is more geared to capital flows than to trade flows. Multi-year swaps involve management of not only exchange risk, but long-term interest rate risk and credit risk.

Because forward rates for year one, year two, year three, and so forth are difficult to calculate with any degree of certainty, the counterparties usually don't try to do so. Rather, they simply exchange currencies at the spot rate and service each other's debt. At the end of five years, they just re-exchange the same amount at the original spot rate. The difference between spot and forward rates is, after all, approximately the difference between the interest rates. As long as the holder of the currency pays the interest which that currency earns, he is automatically compensating for the differences between the spot and forward rates. There is a credit risk involved in doing this because the counterparties service the other's debt by making periodic interest payments between themselves, rather than to each other's lender. The loan obligation remains the borrower's. The lender, be it a bank, a buyer of commercial paper, or an investor in corporate debentures, is often not even aware that the swap has taken place.

Any two interest rates—relative bond yields, for example—can be used. The rates can be fixed or floating, or they can be fixed for one party and floating for the other, with each retaining the initial terms of the loan or swapping them along with the currency. One counterparty may have a higher or lower credit rating than the other. The higher-rated company pays a discount or the lower-rated company pays a premium, which is subtracted or added to the interest payments between them to equalize the rating. Options can be included (the technical term is *embedded*). For example, a party paying a floating rate may want to put a ceiling on the liability. He can purchase an interest rate call option, written by the counterparty and made part of the agreement, with a strike price corresponding to the interest rate ceiling. Both calls and puts can be embedded to establish a "collar" (both a ceiling and a floor). No matter how structured, the swap vehicle can provide an agreement tailored to fit both parties. Assume, for the sake of simplicity, that both loans are made at a floating Eurorate, by which the coupon yields of the five-year Eurobonds—two Eurobonds are used, each denominated in one of the currencies-are swapped periodically over a period of five years. Diagrams A, B, and C of Figure 5-17 show how this occurs.

Figure 5-17: Five-Year Swap

Initial transaction at spot

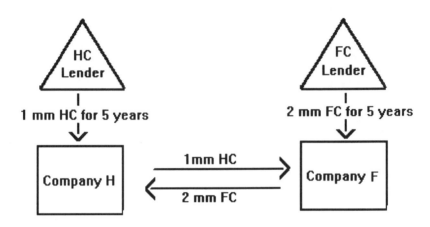

Semi Annual Interest Payments
Twice a Year for 5 Years

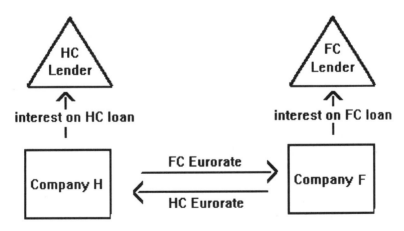

continued on next page

Figure 5-17: Five-Year Swap, *con't.*

Final Transaction at Initial Spot Rate

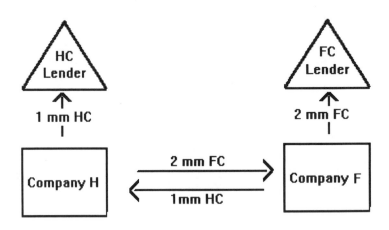

As experience in structuring swaps accumulates, new techniques are introduced for the sake of efficiency. For example, both counterparties do not necessarily have to keep crossing checks in the mail. If the amounts that each owes the other are perfectly equal, the payments will cancel each other out. Very likely, one party will owe more than the other on each payment due date. Only one, then, is required to remit a payment equal to the difference.

The swap can even be accomplished without an initial currency exchange between the parties. It may be more efficient for each to go directly to the interbank and make the exchange as a spot transaction. Then, only the debt service is swapped, not the currency itself. In the same manner, the final re-exchange can also be eliminated simply by reversing the initial spot transaction in the interbank. Stripped of all but the essentials, the swap agreement may stipulate a spot rate that both parties agree to for the initial and final swaps. (Again, this rate is usually the same for both swaps. Why try to guess the spot exchange rate five or ten years out?) Such an agreement requires payments to be made on a periodic basis, with the one who owes the difference at each remittance date making the payment (see Figure 5-18). There is also a final compensation payment from one to the other. This compensates for the difference between the actual market rate at which the final exchange takes place and the agreed upon rate.

Figure 5-18: Currency Swap

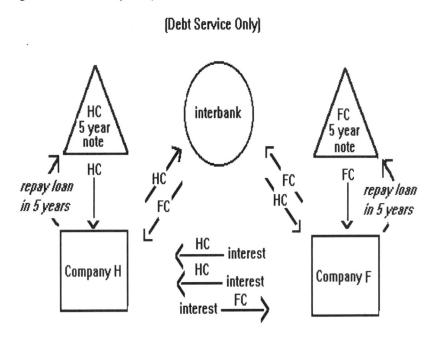

[Debt Service Only]

periodic payment of interest difference

5 years later ...

Final compensation payment to replicate original spot rate

Strategic Exposure

Managing exposure from a strategic standpoint is the epitome of "high finance." To do so, all facets of the problem must be thoroughly understood. Many of us in the financial industry are not be in a position to offer currency swaps for hedging purposes or to undertake operating strategies on behalf of our clients. Most brokers and dealers probably will not be involved in adjusting procedures for collecting receivables and making payables. Still, it is important to know what types of risks your prospects or clients face and the ways in which those risks can be managed.

This point should be emphasized: regardless of your contribution to the client's currency management program, you should have a working knowledge of all forms of exposure, and the tools for handling them. It is the old caveat, "know your customer," or, in this case, your customer's business. This is how you become a credible source in the eyes of your client, and how you become a major player in the game. The goal is for you to become a valuable asset to your client's currency management program.

The Currency Management Program

Many companies manage their currency exposure on a case by case basis. When they contract in Deutsche marks, British pounds, or whatever, they call their broker or banker and ask him or her how to hedge the risk. When the exposure no longer exists, the hedge comes off, and that is the end of currency management until the next time around.

Other companies use what we might refer to as the "ONo" management technique. The treasurer enters a foreign currency transaction in the journal. He does nothing else until one day when he picks up the business news and glances at the markets. "Oh No," he exclaims, "I'm losing my shirt." At that point, he places an urgent phone call to the broker or the banker.

This handbook advocates a different method: the management of currency exposure from a strategic level. Remember that *strategic* currency exposure is defined as a *perception* rather than a specific risk; a way of viewing exposures that envelopes *all types*. From this perspective, the company can determine how its *total* exposure affects company value, both in the present and in the future.

A strategic exposure management program is best constructed by stepping away from the action so there is no immediate pressure to "do something quick" about an existing position. It is easier to conceptualize in a relaxed atmosphere. You, as a broker or dealer, benefit more in the long run when you promote this type of approach. The continuity you can build into a strategic management program helps prevent the company from shopping around for the lowest commission or spread each time a new exposure crops up. The problem with selling a strategic management program, however, is figuring out how to capture the interest of a corporate financial manager when there is no immediate crisis to fix. The solution is the foreign exchange survey.

Preparing the Survey

There are five areas to consider when managing currency exposure strategically. These are:

1. the company,
2. the exposures,
3. a management team,
4. an information management system, and
5. corporate policy.

The first two concerns—the company and the exposures—require careful analysis to design an effective program incorporating the remaining three. This analysis can take the form of a foreign exchange survey. Depending on the prospect, a survey of this type can range from a one-hour interview with the financial manager to a full-blown project demanding weeks of effort. Upon completion, a foreign exchange survey should include a written analysis of the company's objectives, an analysis of the current and projected exposures, conclusions regarding the actual and potential impact of these exposures on the corporate objectives, and a statement regarding the possible solutions. The foreign exchange survey, conducted on behalf of the prospect or client, can be a powerful sales tool as long as the following conditions are met:

1. The survey must be of perceived value to the company. In other words, the company must be sold on the advantages of having a survey undertaken, even when there are no current exposures on the books; therefore, the first step is to develop an effective marketing proposal that extolls the benefits of the survey as a stand-alone product.

2. There should be no strings attached. The corporate manager must know that he or she is free to take your survey findings upon completion, and to bid you thanks and good bye. There should no pressure to open an account as you hand over the findings, otherwise, the survey appears to be simply a sales tool, which diminishes its value in the eyes of the corporate manager. The best way to establish value, if your firm's policy allows it, is to charge for the effort put into it. It is a well-known fact that the perception of value is often in the price of the product. If your company's policy prohibits charging for a survey, consider working with a local

accounting or consulting firm, and have that firm charge for it. It still opens the door for you because you can recommend the survey and be there as the results are presented.

3. The foreign exchange survey must be worth your effort. Again, you must present it without strings, but your time is valuable and must be paid for. This is another reason to charge for the survey. Alternatively, you might provide a survey at no charge if you are quite sure you will receive the prospect's future business without making it a condition. There are obvious measures you can take to protect your interests. For example, you would only solicit business from a company exposed in the currencies that you can trade. Also, the potential volume of business should determine the amount of time you are willing to commit. If you are prospecting a company that deals in tradable currencies, but does no more than $2 million worth of business overseas annually through letters of credit, you may not wish to spend more than an hour or so, note pad in hand, with the treasurer. You may put in a few hours at your desk organizing the information in a manner that leads to realistic conclusions and recommendations. You may or may not charge for this, depending on your relationship with the prospect. If, on the other hand, you put several weeks of effort into a foreign exchange survey for a multinational corporation with worldwide operations (surveys on this scale can take six months or more) you most certainly need to be well compensated with either hard or soft dollars.

The Questionnaire

Certain procedures must be followed to give value to the finished product. First, there is a questionnaire prepared in which background information is gathered. This is where the near-term and long-term goals and objectives of the company are determined, and how they may be impacted by foreign exchange exposure. Then, identify the exposures. Also, take a reading on the company's "risk profile." This helps in determining which management techniques are most suitable for the client. Finally, analyze the information gathered and report the findings and recommendations.

The information obtained using the questionnaire should give a detailed picture of the company and sufficient data to draw conclusions and recommendations. In Figure 6-1 are examples of pertinent questions for this survey. Not every question pertains to every prospect, and neither is this list intended to be all-inclusive. It illustrates, however, the type of information you are after.

Figure 6-1: Questionnaire for Foreign Exchange Survey

General information: *(Information in this section helps you "steer your way around" inside the organization. Identifying a contact person is your first priority, preferably a person who is sold on hedging and is aware of office politics and corporate culture.)*

Include company name, address, phone number; type of organization (corporation, partnership, proprietorship, or other); location of plants and facilities; names of officers and the organizational chart; name of the contact person and the best times to reach him or her. A copy of the corporate charter or bylaws should be obtained to determine if there are restrictions on trading futures or options.

Industry information: Determine the industry (what is the standard industrial classification [SIC])? Is the industry seasonal or cyclical? Does it comprise technical and proprietary products, or services, or is this a commodity-type business? Does the industry involve the manufacture, purchase, or distribution of consumer products, retrofit equipment, original equipment, or something else?

Product or service information: Take a close look at the product line, everything from the sourcing of raw materials to packaging and shipping. Where are production facilities located? How are parts inventories sourced, transported, and stored? How are they financed? Are components sub-assembled elsewhere? What about labor cost? Is this a bench work, contract, salary, or hourly operation? Which currencies denominate the products' cost base? If a service is involved, how is it paid for?

Market information: Where are the markets? Who are the customers? How is the product sold; by jobber, distributor, wholesaler, retailer? Are there offshore marketing units such as joint ventures or subsidiary operations? In which currencies are price sheets denominated? How about receivables? Revenue streams? What about marketing agreements—are franchise fees, licenses, or royalties involved?

This area requires an understanding of market economics. What is the company's pricing policy in each market region? Does it have an exclusive market niche? How price sensitive or elastic is the product?

Figure 6-1: Questionnaire for Foreign Exchange Survey, *cont'd..*

Competitive information: Certain market data concern the company's competitive position; for example, the company's market share should be ascertained. Who are its closest competitors? What differentiates the product line from those of the competition? Who is the price leader, or is price not a major factor? Where are competitive products produced? Which currencies are used for invoicing? Does the competition engage in any known foreign currency management strategies?

Financial information: The survey should include a review of the balance sheet and income statement. All transactional or translation exposure should be identified. How flexible is the company with regard to financial adjustments; for example, if accounting or cash flow exposures are handled at several levels of the operation, can they be consolidated by treasury for central management? How quickly, how often, and how economically can product price sheets be changed? How flexible is company policy concerning sourcing or purchasing? In relation to international marketing, what type of trade finance package is available to the company or its customers?

Risk profile: This is an analysis of risk tolerance levels. "Tolerance" is a subjective attribute, of course, which measures personal attitudes; therefore, you will want to define the attitudes toward various types of risks held by the corporate decision makers, the CEO, the CFO, and the COO. The best way to do this (really, the only way) is by asking. A separate questionnaire can be developed and submitted for this purpose. You want to know how they perceive various types of foreign currency exposure. Are they more troubled by operating exposure or by accounting exposure? What about their attitudes and understanding regarding concepts such as hedge burden, leverage, and derivatives?

To create an effective risk profile, questionnaire include questions about the executives' personal investments. Find out, for example, if they ever traded commodities or options, or whether their investments are strictly limited to treasury bonds, or something in between. Determine, also, if there have been any previous undertakings in corporate hedging for commodities or financials, and if so, the results of the actions taken.

Goals and Objectives: Finally, a foreign exchange survey cannot be effective without taking future plans into consideration. Where does the company want to be next year? How about in five or ten years? Is it aggressive, growth oriented, or defensive in nature? Are there plans for new product introductions, joint ventures, or acquisitions? Are there new sourcing or international trade efforts on the drawing board?

The Analysis

The next stage is to analyze the information gathered. Here is where you incorporate the information regarding the operations, transactions, and corporate objectives with an analysis of the currencies in which the company operates. You identify the risk, in dollar amount, and report the results, along with suitable recommendations. The procedure used to determine risk in each category of exposure is fairly straight forward. First, identify the currencies that denominate exposed positions. Next, measure the exposure in dollar value. Then, measure the degree of foreign currency volatility that can be expected. (This refers to the volatility of nominal exchange rates. Changes in real exchange rates that produce operating exposure require an examination of comparative economic and political conditions-a task for the fundamental research department.)

Value at Risk

Obviously, there is no way to determine whether any given exposed position will generate a profit, a loss, or just remain at its current dollar value. You can, however, assign probabilities of value change. There are several analytical tools for finding such probabilities. *Value at Risk*, or VAR is one tool growing in popularity. Used primarily for institutional investment portfolios, it can be easily adapted to exchange rate volatility.

VAR is *quantified* by a measurement of *standard deviations*. A standard deviation, by definition, is the "dispersion of observations from the mean observation." In other words, unless a currency price is immobilized at a fixed point (the mean observation), it can be expected to move back and forth from that point. By convention, the point used is the previous market close. A unit of standard deviation equals the expected variance, or price range, from *each previous close* over a given amount of time.

As an example, assume that during the last two years, the British pound moved back and forth from the previous close to the next day's opening about two cents, on an average, every trading day; therefore, a two-cent move in either direction is the *overnight volatility* of the British pound (see Figure 6-2). We also know that, every so often, the pound makes sudden large overnight moves of four cents or more. What is the probability that the pound will move more than four cents in one direction between tonight's close and tomorrow's opening?

Figure 6-2: Value at Risk (VAR)

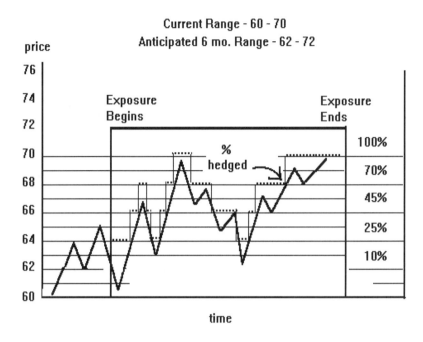

To determine this, assume that the movements are completely random with regard to direction. Plotting the distance of the price move from one trading day to the next, all of the chart points should fall within the area under a bell curve. Because the *expected* change of value can be expressed as the standard deviation of this curve, one standard deviation is equal to two cents from the close of the previous day. By definition, approximately 95% of the area under a bell curve is contained within *two standard deviations*; therefore, there is no more than a 5% chance that an overnight move will exceed four cents in either direction from the previous close. Within these parameters, four cents is the maximum value at risk. In other words, our VAR is (no more than) four cents based on a 95% confidence interval, when analyzed with a two year period of historical market data and assuming a normal distribution curve.

Of course, when assigning risk values to exposed positions, the previous close can be defined on a monthly, quarterly, or even annual bar chart. The expected variance from one quarter to the next would be quite different from the expected variance from one day to the next. After determining the U.S. dollar value of the foreign currency position and the expected variance, or standard deviation, for a given duration, you will know the change of value that probably will occur in the exposed position over time. This works well for transaction exposures with finite values and durations. It can also be used for ongoing cash flow exposure. For cash flow, however, an exposure duration must be chosen, such as monthly exposure, quarterly exposure, semi-annual exposure, and so forth.

Findings and Recommendations

The presentation of findings and recommendations might be made in spread sheet or chart form. The volatility of the currencies denominating assets and liabilities or revenue and expenses serves as a bench mark for the approximate dollar amount at risk. These values can be entered in a probability curve approximating the volatility curve of the currency.

The results of the survey lead to a recommendation of how the company can manage its exposures most effectively, considering its future goals, objectives, and risk profile. Sometimes the survey shows that the company has no significant risk and the best recommendation is to stay the course. Market transactions for hedging purposes carry their own costs and risks. In some smaller companies, hedging is simply not advisable. A survey is just as valuable if the findings show that the company is doing just fine the way things are. It may be a relief to management to have that confirmed. In the future, when revenues or sales increase to the extent that hedging becomes a viable consideration, your efforts—and expertise—will be remembered. Meanwhile, the amount you charged for the survey helps ensure that your time is not spent in vain and that your conclusions are not biased for your own gain.

If exposures are significant, the findings should include recommendations on how to manage them by hedging. Before looking for hedging solutions, however, make sure that there are no counteracting exposures that offset each other. Significant correlations between currencies often create such "natural hedges." For example, an asset denominated in Deutsche marks and a liability denominated in Swiss francs may offset each other if you find a strong correlation between the currencies, as has been the case historically.

The Currency Management Team

You have just completed a foreign exchange survey for an international wholesaler. It reveals substantial accounting or cash flow exposure. The corporate decision makers will consider hedging with futures or options, and you are called in to help set up the hedging program. What is the next step?

Corporate hedging is not a one man show. From a strategic perspective, the impact of currency fluctuations, or the results of managing them, is not felt only in the corporate treasury. Because every exposure—accounting, cash flow, and operating—is only a single facet of an interactive business climate, you must be aware of all departments affected. These can include product engineering, manufacturing, marketing, and sales, as well as finance.

Because of the interdepartmental nature of currency exposure, the most effective solutions are derived from a team effort. Managers of each function impacted by foreign exchange should be queried for input, if they have not been already during the survey. The follow-up to the survey, then, is to solicit the development of a task force or management team. This team will be responsible for developing a program and the policy for implementing it. Ideally, the team will not disband once the program is up and running, but will remain intact to oversee and monitor the progress.

Is a team always necessary? No, probably not. If the exposure is transient and not pervasive, you and the treasurer can devise a hedge strategy, carry it out, and be done with it; but as soon as currency management becomes an ongoing part of the business, or whenever risks other than limited transactional exposures exist, working with an interdepartmental team is the best way to manage it.

Team members

Who belongs on the currency management team? You do, for one. If you have come this far, you probably will be providing transaction services. You may also be the source of the market, economic, and financial information required on an ongoing basis to keep the hedging strategy on track. One of your most important functions will be education. The members of the team must understand the concepts involved. You are the catalyst in conveying this knowledge. In this regard, your most effective forum is the seminar, either in-house or public, which all team members are urged to attend. Two key points to remember for the seminars: (1) bring plenty of visual aids and graphics, such as charts, overlays, and slides, and (2) leave the technical jargon at home.

Another team member will be your contact person. You need to maintain regular contact with one person in the corporation throughout program development, someone who will guide you through the intricacies of company politics. This is especially crucial when dealing with personnel from several departments. Your contact person will most often be the treasurer, or someone acting in a financial management capacity. You two probably will lead the effort in team formation.

A third member should be the corporate accountant or someone familiar with hedge accounting and taxation issues. Others on the team should include individuals in a position of authority from every department or function affected by either currency exposure or by the management of currency exposure.

The last essential person on the team is the senior manager. The presence of senior management is absolutely crucial. It will make the difference between success and failure. Corporate decision-makers do not decide to do things they do not understand, and very few have a good grasp of currency hedging techniques. Not surprisingly, considering the scope of this effort, forming a team requires a great deal of diligent salesmanship. This is another reason for maintaining close touch with your contact person. He or she also serves as your coach, pointing out ways to successfully sell the team concept to those who must get involved and become committed.

Seven Reasons for a Management Team

The actual number of team members, of course, depends upon what is feasible for the particular company. Each situation is different. Company 'A' may have a minimum transactional exposure that remains fairly constant. Company 'B' may have large, fluctuating cash flows and operating exposures in half-a-dozen currencies. The team for Company 'A,' may consist of the assistant treasurer and you, who get together for lunch periodically whenever time allows. For company 'B,' the team may consist of ten or more people for whom the conference room is reserved on the first Wednesday of every month. Regardless of the size and scope, the importance of currency management as a team effort cannot be overstated. The following statements summarize the importance of the team approach:

1. Strategic currency exposure measures the impact of foreign exchange in all areas of the company, including accounting, treasury, manufacturing, marketing, and logistics such as purchasing and distribution. No single individual can be expected to know with certainty the impact of currency moves in all areas.

2. The successful management of foreign currency exposure may draw on a wide range of expertise. No one person can remain on

top of transaction costs and procedures, order entry techniques, record keeping, hedge accounting, tax implications, impact of exchange rates versus interest rates, the latest economic indicators, market and technical analysis, and exposure analysis.

3. Developing a currency management program requires a healthy dose of coordination, and cooperation. If futures or options play a part in it, risk disclosure statements and account forms need to be signed. Up-to-date financial statements are required to open accounts. The brokerage firm or bank may want to review a copy of the corporate charter. A corporate resolution may be necessary to amend it, permitting the use of derivatives for hedging purposes. Brokerage firms opening futures accounts usually follow their own procedures of checks and balances by requiring at least two contact persons, one to enter the orders and one to receive the confirmations.

4. Exposures change continuously. It is vital to stay on top of the exposures that exist today and those coming down the pike tomorrow. Knowing what sales are pending, what investments are under consideration, what purchase agreements are being negotiated, and what new marketing plans are being formulated requires a constant interchange of information on an interdepartmental basis.

5. Before a currency program can get off the ground, it must be "bought" by senior management. Because the program often takes form at the mid-management level, an executive officer or manager must be brought in at some point. It is not unusual for two months to one year to elapse before the an executive committee approves of a hedging program brought before it.[1] The sooner senior management understands what is being proposed, the better (and faster) the chance for approval.

6. Hedging often produces hedge losses (the "hedge burden"). This is expected. It cannot be otherwise because hedges shield the company from foreign exchange losses *and* profits by offsetting them with profits *and* losses. Hedge profits are universally accepted by all. Hedge losses are a different matter. Try telling the chief operating officer of a division—one who is not a member of the currency management team—that his performance over budget won't result in bonuses after all because the excess was due to shifts in foreign exchange that were, well, all hedged away. Hedge losses must be expected, and accepted, *before* they occur.

7. Having two or more team members involved in the day-to-day management is a security measure. One way for a company to make headlines in the financial news is to assign an individual the task of hedging currencies, furnish him with a desk, a quote machine, and a phone, tell him to go at it, and then leave him to his own devices. No trader enjoys running up to his or her boss and exclaiming, "I just dropped another $70,000 today." Many will not. Soon, no one inside the company except the trader and the broker know the amount of profits or losses accruing.

It is easy to hide a running loss when no one is looking over your shoulder. Fear plays a role. The broker fears the loss of the account and the corporate trader fears the loss of his standing and perhaps his job. This type of management program has a good chance of ending with the CEO standing miserably in front of the cameras, describing a multimillion dollar loss in derivative trading and vowing "never again."

The Information Management System

An integral part of any currency management program involves the manner in which information is gathered, processed, and reported. The initial gathering of information can easily be a six month task. Monitoring, coordinating, and revising this amount of data requires a systematic approach. A cash management system is similar, and, in fact, it may be feasible to incorporate cash management and information reporting into one system. The exact nature of the reporting system depends on the program methods and objectives. Essentially, there are four considerations when designing an information reporting system:

1. What information needs to be reported and to whom?
2. Who needs to report it?
3. How often should it be reported?
4. How will it be transmitted?

The core requirement of any information system pertains to hedge accounting. The company must be able to identify, on a moment's notice, which exposed positions are matched to which hedge positions and the financial results produced by the match.

Toward this end, some of the information to be updated on a continuing basis might include:

1. Payables and receivables
2. Information on payer or payee
3. Invoicing dates and currency of invoice
4. Bank balances in all countries
5. Currency deposits and ready assets in all countries
6. Borrowing and lending fees and services in countries of operation
7. Ready methods of repatriating funds
8. Latest valuations of fixed assets and long-term liabilities
9. Latest budget projections
10. Pending sales and purchases
11. Inventory denominated in foreign currencies

Certain market information should also be incorporated on an ongoing basis. The specifics required depend on the hedging techniques employed; practically all include current data in the following areas:

1. Exchange rates
2. Interest rates
3. Updated price charts (daily, weekly, and monthly)
4. Current price trends
5. Economic indicators and econometric input*
6. Fundamental and technical market analysis*

Usually the most difficult part of creating an information reporting system is finding the time to do it. Few employees feel they have ample time for their current work load, let alone the time to develop and maintain a project of this magnitude. Updating data is a daily, weekly, or monthly task, depending on what's to be updated. Maintaining an information reporting system may require the use of a consultant or two, or even additional in-house staffing. The job is time consuming and can be

---

*Certain hedge models only

seen as drudgery. On the positive side, it is not at all complicated. No advanced skills are required to compile the information. Revised figures for sales projections, expenses, etc., can be reviewed by the head of the appropriate department or division before being released to the network. Forms devised for this purpose should be kept as simple as possible. A software spreadsheet such as Microsoft Excel™ works quite well. Whatever form it takes, the information should be easily transmittable by fax or computer.

You can play a vital role in the information management system. Again, the size of the account dictates to a large extent how much time you commit to this. Setting aside fifteen or twenty minutes a week for a "round table" phone conference is certainly not unreasonable. This time can be used to review the latest news and reports influencing the foreign currency markets.

Writing Corporate Policy

One of the currency management team's first priorities is to write a policy manual. Here is where all the information from the foreign exchange survey and input from the team members come together. There are several considerations involved in policy formation. Certain qualifications must be met. First and foremost, successful currency management must:

1. be consistent with corporate philosophy and objectives;

2. incorporate models within acceptable risk parameters;

3. be transparent;

4. be cost effective;

5. operate effectively with available resources; and

6. undergo stress-testing on a regular basis.

Let's look at each of these in detail.

Corporate Objectives

Begin writing policy by defining the program objectives. What, precisely, is this currency management program suppose to do? Whatever its purpose, it must be *explicit* and *in writing*. Many programs fall flat because the purpose is left muddled, and then changes along with the market. If the program is to protect profits, then all hedging procedures, tools, and techniques must be developed with that focus. If, on the other hand, the program is to *produce* profits, an entirely different set of management techniques is required, with an eye more toward the market than toward exposure. The main idea may be neither of these. Instead, it may be to identify and lock in a dollar amount, with hedging used as a price discovery mechanism. Perhaps the program is to function as part of a cash management system for coordinating far-flung receivables and payables in one currency under one department. Each of these goals dictates that the program be developed in a specific manner. This calls for the development of a hedge model.

The Hedge Model

An effective "hedge model" may be defined as a pre-determined course of action within acceptable risk parameters which furthers corporate goals and objectives. If, for example, the decision is made to adjust receivables and payables by leading and lagging, the model might stipulate that whenever a currency begins an upward trend, payables denominated in that currency will be paid within 5 days of notice, rather than 30 days, and receivables in that currency will be extended an additional 30 days before collection. The plan may go on to define the parameters that identify the beginning or the end of a trend, such as a cross over of moving averages. This, then, is a hedge model, an "if this (occurs) then that (occurs)" plan. This can be displayed on a spread sheet or flow chart to review the different pre-planned responses to different market conditions.

A model, then, is a plan of action. We can say that every hedge undertaken incorporates a hedge model; some are effective, some are disastrous. If there is no conscious effort to develop a different one, the hedge will utilize a "default" model, which is frequently too little too late (or too reactive) for best effect.

A corporate risk profile, if one develops from the survey, helps in selecting the hedging model most suitable for a particular type of exposure. Let's assume that company 'A' exports a commodity-type product on a razor thin margin. It has a very low risk tolerance to exposure loss, but a rather high tolerance to hedge burden. Company 'A's primary objective is to protect margin in foreign currency transactions. In this case, the hedge model might well stipulate that all exposure is 100% hedged with futures 100% of the time.

Company 'B' has a different risk profile and a different objective. This company exports a proprietary, high-margin product. Management has a low risk tolerance to exposure loss and hedge burden. The company's objective is to use a hedging program to produce profits. One potential model in this case may be an option program to hedge foreign currency receivables, in which the downside of the currency is protected, and the upside is left unhedged for opportunity gain. The high profit margin is shaved to finance the premiums.

When the objective is to increase profit margin through hedging activity, the risk factor goes up. If opportunity for gain is to be allowed, the hedge program has to move closer to the speculative end of the scale, or the cost of an option premium is exacted to reduce the risk of lost profit opportunity. Assuming risk tolerance levels permit, the most appropriate models for transaction exposure would involve selective hedging techniques such as those in which hedges are placed only when the trend is going in the right direction. Selective hedge models such as the Range Hedge Model, are devised with profit opportunities in mind (see Figure 6-3).

Transparency

An effective currency management program must be transparent. This means that it must be clearly understood by those responsible for its implementation and oversight, as well as those who carry out the day-to-day trading functions. If senior managers approve a hedge model, they must know its possible consequences. A lack of knowledge of hedging procedures, a lack of awareness concerning the market risks involved, or simply not following a policy of ongoing checks and balances may have resulted in some of the following headlines:

- "Barings brought down by futures trader."
- "Proctor & Gamble posts losses of $157 million by virtue of derivatives positions."
- "Atlantic Richfield, the American energy giant, lost some $72 million in financial derivatives in an employee investment fund it manages."
- "Piper Jaffray loses $700 million in a U.S. Government bond fund."

Figure 6-3: Range Hedge Model

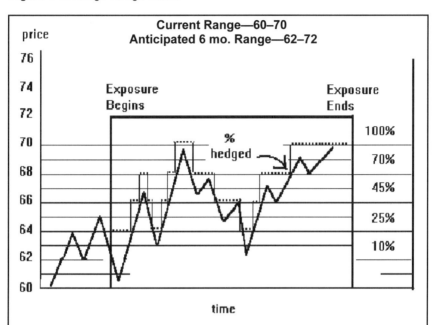

Models may be static or dynamic. The range model is an example of a dynamic hedge strategy. The decision on whether to hedge any given exposure, and to what degree, is a function of the market; therefore, the hedge is continuously under review for revision. A range hedge model has the following characteristics:

Objective:	Locking in the top (or bottom) third of a projected range;
Risk Profile:	Moderate aversion to exposure risk;
Hedge dynamics:	Price driven.

Price levels, rather than levels of exposure, drive the model. Market analysis and forecasting are keys to its success. The first step to setting up this model is the determination of an operating time span. It must not extend beyond the ability to forecast; a three to nine month limit is probably feasible. A range exceeding one year probably is not. The second step is to forecast the most probable price range for the stipulated length of time. Acknowledging the imprecision of forecasting, most models allow prices to exceed the predicted

continued on next page

Figure 6-3: Range Hedge Model, *cont'd.*

range for as much as 10% to 15% of the time; therefore, the range is defined as the ceiling and floor between which the (spot) currency trades 85% to 90% of the time. This flexibility allows room for the sudden price "spikes" characteristic of volatile markets, in which prices trade outside of the range, but soon return.

Once the range has been determined, it is subdivided into, for example, five segments delineating the top 20%, the second 20%, and so on, down to the bottom 20% of the market. The amount of exposure hedged at any moment in time depends on which segment of the range the current price falls into. The objective is to have the greatest amount of an asset (liability) exposure hedged in the top (bottom) 20% of the range, and the least amount hedged in the bottom (top) 20%.

The mechanics are fairly straight forward. Assume that a foreign currency (FC) has been trading between 60 and 70 for the last six months. The current price is 65. Recently, a moderate upward trend has emerged. The consensus is that FC will now trade between 62 and 72 for the next six months. The management team decides that the exposed asset is to be 100% hedged at 72 and 10% hedged at 62, with the percentages increasing or decreasing accordingly as the market moves through the various levels. It is apparent that the positions must be "actively traded" to keep the hedge in line with the market.

- "Metallgesellschaft, the German industrial giant, comes close to receivership after losing nearly $2 billion in derivatives."

- "Orange County loses $1.5 billion from derivatives in investment portfolio."

Directors on the board and the executive officers who report to them read headlines
like these almost daily. A currency management program that doesn't address the issue of security and oversight has slim chance of approval. To build confidence in the program, there are three key elements to keep in mind.

1. Always use "plain vanilla" hedge models unless you are absolutely sure that the company has the expertise to fully understand and manage more complicated derivative strategies.

2. Educate all team members. Assuming you are on the team, this is *your* job, as the expert in the field. Plan and develop seminars and in-house training workshops accordingly.

3. Formulate policy around the concept of *full disclosure*. This means that open positions, unrealized gains and losses, and closed-out trading results must be disclosed in the form of an easy-to-follow report submitted to senior management weekly. It also means that trade confirmations, trade fills, and account information are furnished to someone other than, or in addition to, the individual placing the trades. It also means that policy is written in a manual, copies of the manual are distributed to team members, and at least one person in a position of authority is in charge of maintaining compliance with the stated policy.

Cost/Benefit Analysis

Regardless of the more specific objectives, the corporation considers currency management either to protect the bottom line or to improve it. A currency program that costs more than it can potentially save is worse than no program at all; yet, a surprising number of hedge programs do just that. The first consideration is whether the program makes economic sense before transactions costs. That can be readily determined; if it meets the objectives and the risk is not out of line, it is probably economically feasible. The second question is whether it still makes economic sense when transactions costs are included. This is somewhat more difficult to ascertain. Hedging a currency that hasn't moved more than 2 or 3% against the dollar for more than a year may not, on the surface, look like an economical move when commissions, spreads, management fees, and other program costs are taken into account; but what if the fiscal policy of the country takes a sudden turn? Or, overnight, the struts are kicked out from beneath a solidly pegged currency? In an assembly line fashion, financiers in Malaysia and Thailand borrowed US dollars, converted them into ringetts and baht, and then into high-rise apartments and office buildings that dotted the landscape. They felt, perhaps, like holiday boaters rowing down a prosperous river of commerce, never noticing until too late the distant roar in front of them. It was the sound of their currencies going over the edge.

Not only the program, but the specific trading tactics employed by the program must be justifiable from a cost standpoint. Perhaps it makes sense to get out of the market every night, or when a government report is imminent, and then re-establish the position. There are brokers who advocate "spreading the position" in the face of every uncertainly that comes down the pike; however, if these tactics were suggested for a hedge model, the broker would have to be very persuasive to convince a savvy management team that the purpose is for anything other than churning the account.

Perhaps the most difficult model to cost-justify is the option strategy. Let's face it. Option premiums can be as difficult to sell as insurance premiums, which is what they are. Still, for certain exposures, especially those such as outstanding project bids which are tentative in nature, an option spread or a combination strategy—in which premium costs are reduced by premiums collected—may be the only cost-effective way to go.

Appropriate Resources

The types of resources available for currency management should match the scope of the exposures to be managed and the techniques and models selected for the program. If your firm offers full client service, complete with technical and fundamental research departments, you may be able to provide all the analytical services required. Your services can make up the core of the information management system. It is then incumbent upon you to transmit the research to the right people in a timely manner. Possibly, a weekly phone conference would be appropriate.

If you specialize in fast, economical transaction service, but have no research facilities, the corporate management team may want to enlist a CTA or hedge manager to furnish technical or fundamental research. The information provided must be comprehensible to those who will act upon it. For example, if option strategies are to be part of the model and no one on the management team knows what "delta hedge" means, either an options specialist should be brought on board—one who can explain options in layman's terms—or the program should be changed to another format. Simply put, the information required must not be of such a technical nature that no one inside the corporation understands it. This harkens back to the transparency of the program. Senior managers must not only be informed, they must *understand.*

Outside Management

There is an exception to the team concept. Only individuals can trade effectively; committees cannot. The actual trading is not, therefore, a team effort. A single individual must be given the authority to trade. The trader may be a company employee or someone outside. Perhaps you do the trading through power of attorney, as the broker, dealer, or advisor. You will have knowledge and expertise that is not necessarily disseminated to other members of the team. It is not critical that each member of the management team know the technical reasons behind every trade or, indeed, what the trading position is on a daily basis; however, *someone* in the company should know. Delegating trading authority does not alleviate the management team's responsibility to know *in principle* the reason behind the hedge tactics that are being used. Even more importantly, each member should know the corporate policy of currency management in detail. Any member of the team should be able to stand in front of an executive committee and explain, without perspiring, the reason for that last $100,000 margin call.

It is not critical for a company that employs an option hedging strategy to have an in-depth knowledge of option delta values if an outside option specialist is managing the positions, but there are limits to how far into unknown territory a company can venture when its net worth is at stake. For example, a "black box" (a proprietary system that generates buy and sell orders using undisclosed technical parameters) is probably not a suitable model for a currency management program; no team member wants to have to explain to the board of directors how a "secret trading system" just cost the company 10% of its last quarter's earnings.

Stress Testing

Producing stressful scenarios to determine how the hedge model handles them is known as stress testing. It is an analysis using "what if" situations. What if the market goes up or down *x* percent? How do we respond using this hedge model? An effective model should incorporate a pre-determined course of action for any conceivable event. You can set up a stress test on a spread sheet, or on a legal pad with the appropriate columns drawn. No matter how simple or elaborate the test, imagination is the key element. Conjure up various "worst case" scenarios and note the response dictated by the model.

Risks of Hedging

Worst case scenarios encompass the inherent risks that are a part of any hedging strategy. These risks can be categorized as follows:

- *Political risk*—When a position is placed on a foreign futures or options exchange, the positions are subject to the laws of that country. A political change could affect the position. The worst case scenario would be one in which the contract terms of a profitable hedge position suddenly became unenforceable or declared null and void.

- *Transfer risk*—The delivery of a foreign currency in accordance with the specifications of the contract is prevented or restricted by the government that issues that currency. This occurred with the Mexican peso futures contract trading on the CME in the late 1970s. More recently, the government of Malaysia threatened to change the rules of foreign exchange involving its currency in an attempt to quell speculative selling.

- *Settlement risk*—Settlement risk is similar to transfer risk, except that the counterparty is another trader, market, or exchange. Settlement is not performed in accordance with the contract because of a dispute between the parties.

- *Credit risk*—This has the same result as settlement risk, but is caused by the counterparty defaulting due to insolvency. Private counterparty hedge agreements, such as OTC hedges and currency swaps, have no clearing facility. Neither do bank forward transactions, a selling point for the futures broker.

- *Legal risk*—The hedge is declared unenforceable because it is not found to be a legal instrument; for example, a court may conclude that the agreement constitutes fraud because of a lack of disclosure (witness the legal activities surrounding derivative losses of late), or a foreign government may find that the hedge agreement does not conform to its laws.

- *Market risk*—This is the risk that market action will create a loss. In a bona fide hedge transaction, market action theoretically has no impact on the bottom line. In the real world, market action may have a great deal of impact. Many hedge programs fail because management cannot tolerate the growing losses from the hedge position, even though the exposed position is doing very nicely, thank you. *It is extremely important* that this "stress" is tested in the model because the chances of its occurring are so high.

Another type of market risk has nothing to do with tolerance levels. This is the risk of a change in correlation between the exposed and hedged positions, known as *basis risk*. In the worst case scenario, both positions lose money. This risk is most evident when one currency or currency derivative is being used as a proxy to offset an exposure in a different currency.

- *Liquidity risk*—The risk here is that the market simply dries up, making it virtually impossible to liquidate a hedge position at a fair market price or, under extreme conditions, at any price. Currency swaps and other private counterparty agreements for which there is no developed secondary market carry a high degree of liquidity risk.

- *Operations risk*—This is the risk of error which, as brokers are well aware, is the most common and often the most costly of all— the ever-present potential for errors such as entering a "buy" for a "sell." I suspect that some of the headlines reproduced above are the end result of what started as a simple operation error. A small but significant loss-producing error is concealed by the individual who tries to trade his or her way out of it. It grows from there.

Trading Rules

It is becoming increasingly evident that the corporate currency manager and the currency speculator have much more in common than either are willing to own up to (the speculator considering himself a breed apart, and all). Both are at risk of financial loss in unpredictable markets. The cash exposure carried by the corporation is no different from the market exposure of the speculator. They are managed in a similar fashion. Paradoxically, the risk disappears for both when the currency manager gets into the market and the speculator gets out; both assume exposure risk when the hedger steps out of the market and the speculator steps in.

This being the case, imagine a scenario in which one currency manager and one currency speculator transact with each other, each hoping to profit from a trade in which only one will. If the speculator is seasoned, he is probably trading as mechanically and impassively as he knows how, aided by a system that's calling the shots. If he is doing it right, he planned the trade in advance, and now he's trading the plan. The currency manager should do the same.

It is to the currency manager's advantage, therefore, to know the rules of the game. They are listed below in no particular order. Most, but not all, were developed by speculators who validated them by painful experience. Others pertain specifically to hedging. They will all serve the currency manager equally well.

1. *Do not "Texas hedge."* A "Texas hedge" is not a hedge at all—it is speculation. Unless the market exposure is in the opposite direction from the cash exposure, the company is not hedging. Also, to the extent that the exposure is over-hedged or under-hedged, the company is speculating, either in cash or derivatives.

2. *Be sure of your position.* Simple transactions are obviously long or short, but the more complex a hedge becomes, the less obvious the positions may be. Convoluted option strategies and option-embedded counterparty agreements may be difficult to unravel into component longs and shorts. Thoroughly pick apart all derivative strategies and identify each component by amount, duration, and position.

3. *Calculate your equity balance daily.* Foreign exchange and futures accounts should be marked to the market daily. It is all too common for huge losses to accrue undetected until it is too late to salvage the program.

4. *Do not over-leverage.* Figure out the worst case scenario and make sure funds are available to back up the market position if it occurs. In regard to futures positions, delays in meeting margin calls can result in unrealized losses suddenly becoming realized without the currency manager's knowledge. Recognizing this, most brokers and dealers have standing instructions to liquidate an overdue margin position immediately, at the market, with or without the client's approval.

5. *Do not lift hedges prematurely simply to stem a loss.* If the hedge is sound, liquidating it to cut a loss will leave the exposure vulnerable to a price reversal. There is nothing worse than getting out of the market with a realized loss only to see additional losses accumulate in the exposed position as prices suddenly go the other way.

6. *Do not lift hedges prematurely simply to take a profit.* It's tempting to take profits, especially after agonizing through a string of trading losses. It is tempting to want hedging positions to produce

profits, even more than cash positions. It is easy to rationalize profit-taking believing that the market has gone too far, too fast. It seems so certain that there will be an opportunity to re-establish the hedge at a better price. Too often, there is no better price. A characteristic of market trends is that they keep going much farther than anyone expects. Hedge profits can quickly dissipate as the now-unhedged exposure generates losses.

7. *Do not carry futures contracts into the last trading date.* Also, do not carry options right up to expiration unless you intend to exercise. Liquidity dries up rapidly during the last weeks before financial instruments go off the board. Illiquid markets can be very difficult to get into or out of at a fair price because very few traders are willing to transact the other side. Carrying the position into the last moments increases significantly the risk of being unable to liquidate. Then you are obligated to exchange the underlying currency, with the added trouble and expense that can entail.

8. *Stress test your model.* This means drawing up a "what if" spread sheet and going through the motions of various worst-case scenarios. Hedge models should be tested for illiquidity, volatility, price extremes, and basis correlation. It is similar to flight simulation practice. With advance preparation, there is less change of panic during the storm.

9. *Do not subscribe to real-time quote streams.* Staring at a stream of prices skyrocketing and falling time after time during the day does not improve either hedging techniques or decision making. What is does do is bring on adrenaline rushes, outbreaks of emotional trading, and stupor. Leave real-time quotes to the day traders and scalpers. They are useless for the vast majority of all hedge programs. Instead, download end-of-day price data, or simply review the action in the Wall Street Journal or other financial newspaper the following day.

10. *Update price charts daily.* Daily, weekly, and monthly price ranges should be charted. Together, they provide a short-term, intermediate-term, and long-term view of price movement, permitting an excellent "feel" for the market. Daily price charts should be updated before the next trading session. There is no better way to stay on top of the market than by updating these charts personally.

11. *Trade only liquid positions.* Whether hedging with futures, options, or forward contracts, stay away from distant or illiquid months unless there is no alternative. Obviously, some derivatives, such as long-term swaps and forwards, are illiquid by nature. Look for ways to offset these hedges with derivatives in correlating markets if it becomes necessary to do so. The ability to quickly liquidate all positions at a fair price should be built into every currency management program.

12. *Liquidate with market orders.* Do not try to play the market after the exposure disappears. Just get out. Doing anything else is simply speculating.

13. *Shop around.* When phoning for a dealer quote, have another dealer on another line. Let each one know you are getting simultaneous quotes. You may be surprised how much the spread narrows in your favor.

14. *Avoid conflicts of interest.* Your broker or dealer may be the most knowledgeable person on your team, but remember that his compensation is based on numbers. Keep it in mind when you consider delegating trading authority to the broker/dealer. This is why the primary qualification to look for in a broker or dealer is ethical behavior.

15. *Avoid Order Miscommunications.* The second leading cause of financial loss in trading the currency markets involves communication errors. The only source of greater loss is market risk itself.

It is surprising how often "buy" and "sell" are inadvertently reversed during a phone conversation with the broker/dealer. In the case of the broker, the transmission process can break down. The broker passes your instructions on. When he is told to "buy ten contracts of March Swiss francs," he writes down those instructions exactly, and forwards them to the floor, where the contracts are purchased for your account. If, however, he has been selling Swiss francs for customers all morning long, and has sell orders scattered across his desk, he may write "sell ten contracts" out of sheer momentum.

Sometimes the confusion results by transacting with both brokers and dealers. Compare their functions. When you instruct your broker to "buy 5 contracts of March Swiss francs, the broker relays your order to the floor, and the contracts are purchased for your account. But when you instruct a *dealer* to "buy 600,000 Swiss francs for March 21," do you mean that the dealer is to buy francs *for* you, or buy francs *from* you? The first constitutes a buy, the second a sell.

The best way to avoid order entry errors is to always have the broker/dealer repeat your instructions back to you. They are supposed to do this as a matter of course, but sometimes neglect to do so during active market conditions, when their minds are racing. You should also tape all conversations with the broker/dealer in case of disputes. They do so for their protection, and you should for yours. Also, make it a point to scrutinize all order and trade confirmations as soon as you receive them.

16. *Keep Track of GTC Orders.* Another all-too-common source of loss is the forgotten order. This is a problem with GTC orders only, since day orders are automatically canceled at the end of each trading session. The loss occurs when a limit or stop order is placed and not filled. The market moves away and you re-enter the order at a different price. If the original order is forgotten and left uncancelled, it remains valid until the market returns to fill it. This is discovered when the manager receives an unexpected confirmation of a trade weeks, or even months, later. (To help alleviate this problem, some exchanges and brokerage firms cancel GTC orders automatically after 30 days, requiring their reinstatement by the customer.)

17. *Support the trader.* This is, perhaps, the most important rule of all. Whether you or someone you authorize makes the day-to-day trading decisions, never engage in Monday morning quarterbacking. Trading is difficult enough, and it is very ego-deflating when the decision produces losses. Intense pressure to always make a profit can lead to paralysis, recklessness, or nondisclosure of a growing loss. These are all roads to financial disaster. The best way to prevent this is to engage in a mechanical style of trading using an appropriate hedge program or model.

CHAPTER 7

Prospecting the Corporate Client*

Everyone in the financial industry is familiar with boiler room operations. They usually go hand in hand with aggressive telemarketing. The operators dial for dollars, promising wealth to anyone who picks up the phone. Brokers and dealers in commodities, penny stock and wildcat drilling rights did not invent this type of deceptive selling, of course, although they may have elevated it to a fine art. This type of selling actually began long before the first batch of snake oil was made ready for bottling. This is "hucksterism," and it is based upon the belief that every sale results in a winner and a loser. If the salesman succeeds in closing the sale, he wins and the buyer loses. If he doesn't succeed in closing the sale, he loses; the buyer wins. Win-lose selling is not an enjoyable way to make a living, nor is it a successful way in the long term.

Consultative Selling

There is another method, called consultative selling. This method is used by all types of salespeople, consultants and non-consultants alike, from counter clerks to diplomats. Consultative salespeople have a few things in common. Their probability of success is high. They are professional. They probably enjoy respect. They often exhibit a sense of high self-esteem. The principle behind consultative selling is simple and basic. It is called *win-win selling*, and it involves a transfer of information from the

---

*Author's note: Although this chapter is written from the perspective of a broker for the broker, the concepts are just as valid for the banker, consultant, advisor, treasurer, or any other financial professional who presents a foreign currency risk management program to corporate senior management

seller to the buyer by which the buyer profits. The consultative salesperson does not try to close a sale until *both parties* win. Both must be better off after the sale than they were before. Furthermore, the win for the buyer is always apparent. The win for the seller is less so, sometimes delayed, but just as sure. The hallmark of consultative selling is "the customer comes first."

How does consultative selling work in the futures industry? John Walsh, who "wrote the book" on how to open futures accounts, states that the most important criterion by which to judge a broker from the client's perspective is credibility. The size of the firm, track record, and commissions are all secondary. The client, as well as the prospect, wants to be able to believe his broker above all else. He becomes a willing buyer only after he knows the broker is genuinely looking for a way for his customer to win. At that point, he believes.

Win-win selling and credibility are two sides of the same coin. Both are absolutely mandatory in the presentation of a currency management program. Hedging currencies is too complex and fraught with its own set of risks to be an "easy sale" unless the buyer has complete confidence in the broker; however, to enjoy maximum success in this field, you must take win-win selling one step further. As the seller, you must often delay your gratification. The client must always win immediately through a reduction of risk, even if his doing so delays the "win" for the broker (generation of commissions). Often, you must advise *against* hedging when you find it is not in the client's best interest. This characteristic of immediate buyer and delayed seller wins leads to the following categorical statement:

> *Unless the broker anticipates building a long term client-consultant relationship, he or she has no business presenting a currency management program to a prospect.*

This is not a statement of ethics, although that certainly is part of it. It is a matter of practicality. For your own success, currency management must be sold as a long-term program, an ongoing policy, a program in which you intend to play a part as long as you and your client remain in business. Developing a currency management program for a one-time commission—a single foray into the markets—is simply not worth your effort.

The First Appointment

Properly nurtured, credibility develops very rapidly between broker and prospect. The first time you meet the treasurer, you will know whether or not he believes you. We've heard that first impressions are lasting. Here, they are critical. If you are found wanting in believability, there will not be a second appointment. In prospecting efforts, you may often experience that the less knowledgeable your listener is about what you have to say, the more interest he will have in you. You are suggesting something that can greatly impact the company's financial condition. You and your proposal will be scrutinized thoroughly.

This is why credibility is so important. Remember that you are asking the company to turn to you for help in determining which derivatives to use, which trades to make, when, for how long, and for how much. A dependency of sorts results—the company hands over to you a certain amount of fiscal control. It would not even consider doing so if your credibility was in doubt. This being the case, how do you gain credibility?

Do Your Homework

Let's start with product knowledge (in reference to your product, not your prospect's). Your role is that of an educator. During your first few contacts with the company, you probably will be talking to people with little more than a passing knowledge of what this is all about. They must depend on your expertise. Your knowledge base should include, of course, the current situation of specific currencies, as well as the dynamics of specific exposures. There is no point in speaking at length on a particular exposure in British pounds if you don't know, within a few points, where the pound is currently trading or what is presently influencing the price. One consultant took great pains during his presentation persuading his audience that he knew all there was to know about the Chinese "Youan." (To no avail, it turned out; "Yuan" is pronounced "won.")

Secondly, you must know your prospect. You need to be familiar with the company's operations *before* your first appointment. Although you may not have detailed information, you should at least know the names of the officers and their positions. You should have some knowledge of the industry and the current business cycle. You should know a little about its main competitors. You most certainly should know what the company produces and sells, and, if possible, where.

Where do you learn these things? Begin with other brokers in your office. A cohort may be in contact with the company with regard to another matter such as pension planning or cash management. Search the internet for the company's web page, or SEC financial reports. Check also with your manager. His function is to know the local market. Perhaps your research department has data on the company. Often, however, you will have to supplement any internal information you gather by going outside. Ask the chamber of commerce about the prospect. Check the local library. You will find a wealth of knowledge in the directory section. If your prospect is a public corporation, call the public relations department and ask them to mail you the latest copy of their annual report. Call the company's marketing department and ask for a product catalog. If you are checking out a position, call the main switchboard and tell whoever answers that you are directing a letter to the person in that position. (It's the truth. If you get the appointment, you should send a follow up letter.) Ask for a spelling of the name, as well as the title. Confirm the correct mailing address, phone, and fax numbers while you're at it.

You have done the homework and set up the appointment. You are now sitting in a conference room at the company's main office, addressing three or four corporate managers whom you met just moments ago. Someone suddenly asks you about a competitive product line that you never heard of. What do you do? First, let's talk about what you *never* do. You do not wing it. If you don't know the answer to an unexpected question, say so. We have all heard the speaker trying to extricate himself by taking a stab at the answer. This is a death knell for any sales presentation at the level we're discussing. Fielding a question without knowing the answer never goes unnoticed. The speaker's credibility immediately plummets. When you don't know the answer then say, "I don't know" or, "I'll find out." It is surprisingly well accepted. When you stand in front of an audience, remember that you are not *really* expected to know *everything*.

Create an Interest

After fifteen tries, you finally convince the secretary of the CEO that you are important enough to be patched through to her boss. He answers the phone and barks "Smith!" or "Jones!" Definitely not a person given to small talk with strangers. You respond by saying (pick one):

(a.)   "Good morning, Mr. Smith. This is Bob Crandell with EZ Bank. I have an idea for reducing the risk of your foreign exchange exposures. When can I stop by to explain it to you?"

(b.)   "Good morning, Mr. Smith. This is Bob Crandell with EZ Bank. Your treasurer, Mr. Green, and I were discussing the feasibility of a foreign exchange survey to determine your company's exposure to currency risk. He asked that I contact you in this regard. Can we meet next week?

Which statement do you think will get a more positive response? The foreign exchange survey is one of the best door openers for prospecting new accounts. It certainly builds credibility; however, it is not without pitfalls. You should not attempt a foreign exchange survey unless it is thoroughly thought out and well executed. It has to be of value to the company. An ill-conceived or unprofessional findings report is worse than useless. Bad advice can be very damaging to the prospect. At the very least, your credibility will take a lethal beating.

If you do not have the time or expertise to prepare a top-notch survey, call in an expert who does, perhaps an accountant or a management consultant familiar with international treasury operations. (Go with him during the interview.) If the prospective company understands the value of the survey, it should have no problem paying the expert for his time. Not only will the results appear more credible, you will also, by association. After all, it is you who presented the concept and initiated the effort.

The Follow-up Proposals

It is rare indeed to open a hedge account on the first appointment. Some risk managers claim that the average time from the initial contact to the signing of the papers is between six months and a year. During that time, you will be meeting with mid-level and senior managers. You may be asked to talk to the executive committee, the bankers, or the attorneys. Sometimes the meeting will be on a one-to-one basis. Other times you will be standing in front of an audience, flip chart beside you and pointer in hand.

The sale, in other words, is not a single event. It is a procession of appointments and meetings. Nor does the sale end with the opening of the account. Now, the company must learn how to use forwards, futures and options in a systematic manner. More selling takes place in different forums with different objectives. In fact, between the time you first initiate contact and the time the company has a detailed currency management program up and running, you will be a familiar enough figure at the company to be mistaken for an employee now and then.

Be prepared, then, to make a series of presentations. Whether they take place over lunch with just the treasurer or in front of a class of marketing and production personnel, these presentations should be consultative in nature and educational in content. Remember that imparting knowledge is the hallmark of consultative sales.

Let's review the various phases of a currency management program that may require the presentation of a proposal in one form or another.

- *The introduction.* Let's say that your first encounter is with the treasurer. You have two primary objectives. The first is to sell yourself as knowledgeable and credible in this area of expertise. The second is to learn about your future client. For this presentation, bring a blank note pad and a list of questions. Don't bring in promotional or other prepared material. You don't want to look like you're selling off-the-shelf solutions. The third objective is to be invited back. If you sell yourself successfully, the treasurer can find a reason for you to return, even if he is not yet convinced about the concept. A foreign exchange survey is one good reason for coming back.

- *The foreign exchange survey.* Depending on the scope of the operation, this may take anywhere from an hour to a few weeks of your time. Let's say the company is a mid-sized manufacturer without extensive foreign operations. A survey of this size might require two to four appointments on-site to gather information. This is the time to ask for a tour of the plant. A tour helps you get a feel for the operation and demonstrates your interest.

- *Presentation of the survey findings and recommendations.* How you handle this depends on the circumstances. You might decide on a full-blown presentation to a group, complete with slides or overheads, or you may decide on an informal work session with your contact person. When the company accepts your findings and is ready to proceed, the way is clear to introduce other proposals or objectives. Any or all of these may need to be presented to the company either formally or informally:

  ➤ Forming a management team

  ➤ Policy and strategy meetings

  ➤ Developing an information management system

  ➤ Developing hedge models

➤ Final approval and sign off

➤ Instruction in trading derivatives

➤ Instruction in market forecasting techniques

➤ Monitoring the program and providing updates

To summarize, selling a currency management program is not a one time event. It is a process that advances step by step. You are introducing a number of objectives which need to be presented and accepted. No matter what you are proposing at any particular moment, or to whom, one thing never changes. You are continuously selling yourself, your firm, and your credibility.

Full Disclosure

There is more to credibility, of course, than a display of knowledge. After all, many hucksters are experts in their field. A credible presentation does not just inform; it informs *honestly*. At some point during the sale, the listeners become convinced that their interests are being fully addressed and have precedence over those of the broker. They reach this point when they realize that the broker is *fully disclosing* all the material facts.

John Walsh, in his ethics training seminars, refers to a particular broker whom he observed in front of an audience of prospective clients. "Most of my clients lose money," she intones, during her opening remarks, "and if you each open an account with me, seven out of ten of you will lose money." She is one of the most successful futures brokers in the business, opening more speculative accounts than many of her cohorts combined. Why? Because she is so believable. There is no question that she fully discloses the facts.

Putting the client's interests first means that you not only understand, but believe in what you are saying. It means that you are as forthright with the negative aspects of hedging as you are with the positive. In the securities industry, anything less than "full and complete disclosure" is construed as an unethical, if not fraudulent, business practice. This includes not only misstatements of fact, but *omission* of facts. (There is no real distinction between the two.) A corporate decision-maker who is not familiar with hedging will be very attentive to what you say and how you say it. Any sign of holding back will almost certainly be noticed, and that will be the end of any chance of approval for your program.

Everyone has heard sales pitches that highlight the advantages and gloss over the disadvantages. A hedge advisor, for example, may propose to a company that it manage its liabilities with long hedge positions. Then he offers examples of hedges that only involve up markets. The examples always result in a hedge profit. Such a biased presentation almost never goes unnoticed. To achieve credibility, the presentation must illustrate examples of up markets *and* down markets. Avoid illustrations that can be construed as less than forthright. When the presentation is peppered with profitable hedge examples, the question in your prospects' minds becomes, "what *else* is he hiding?"

Make sure that everyone has a complete understanding of the risks involved. The idea, of course, is to *reduce* exposure. Explain that hedging does not completely *eliminate* exposure. Sometimes it replaces it with another type. Certain techniques substitute exposure risk for market risk, credit risk, or whatever. Discuss operation risk, basis risk, loss of liquidity, etc. It is far better to disclose these pitfalls up front. Remember that it is not just the rules of hedging you are concerned with. Corporate managers bring their own set of rules to the table. Near the top of the list is "no surprises." When surprises such as unexpected basis fluctuations or liquidity problems occur, it can get quite unpleasant all the way around.

The biggest disclosure problem of derivative hedging concerns leverage. This is totally unnecessary. I strongly recommend presenting all derivative examples as unleveraged transactions. In other words, if it takes 100 futures contracts of Swiss francs to hedge an exposure and the required margin is $290,000, don't create the impression that the company is only risking $290,000. With Swiss francs at 8550, the company would be committing $10,687,500 in francs, and it should be made perfectly clear that this is the amount, in dollars, exposed in the market.

Selling a Track Record?

You may be recommending a trading system as part of your model. Perhaps your system comes with an enviable track record. The *Commodity Futures Trading Commission* (CFTC) requires that any published track record regarding futures contracts includes a disclaimer. This is a statement that "past performance does not guarantee future results." Making a claim to the contrary constitutes fraud according to federal regulations. The CFTC also differentiates between a "real" and a "hypothetical" trading record. The latter contains results that would have occurred if the trades had actually taken place. Both are legitimate representations, but there is an additional caveat included with the use of hypothetical results. A system can be "curve fitted" to include winning trades and exclude losing ones. Whether that same curve will ever recur is anyone's guess. No system yet devised has ever performed consistently in every currency market over significant periods of time. Even if one were found, no claims could be made regarding its *future* performance.

There are a lot of past and current commodity traders around. Some may be on the corporate executive committee or in the board room listening to your presentation. They are well aware of the inflated claims surrounding trading systems. The best advice I can give you is to not even *hint* that you may have a "profitable trading system" for the program. If you do, keep it to yourself.

Some Common Traps

Never forecast the market during a sales presentation. Why? Because you might be risking the whole program on the toss of a coin. This is a major trap. It is often set while you are in the middle of your presentation. Someone around the table innocuously asks what you think the franc or the pound or the peso is going to do in the next two weeks or so. You innocently share your thoughts. It's going to continue up, or head back down, or whatever. You have at least a 50% chance of being wrong. You probably have closer to a 80% to 90% chance of being wrong because the market is going to go up *and* go down *and* go sideways over the near term. The person who queried you doesn't remember the days you are right. He remembers the days you are wrong.

When the buyer discovers that you predicted the market incorrectly, well then, where *else* are you misinformed? What if they had placed company funds on that forecast? "We could have lost a great deal of money," the thinking goes. "Let's take another look at this." (Translation: forget it.) On the average, seven out of ten futures trades go awry. That's 70% of all predictions. An old pro once told me of a technique he used when prospecting for commodity speculators. "Whenever someone tells me about a big position he's holding with another broker," he said, "I furrow my brow and look worried." If you are pressed on this issue, and must respond with a prediction of some sort, use the "straw man" approach. Tell them what some *other* analyst thinks. Set some one else up.

"So You're a Technician"

Once at a prospecting seminar hosted by a commodity trading advisory firm, the speakers took turns describing their technical system to the audience for more than two hours. They were quite wrapped up in the subject, and their enthusiasm was certainly genuine. Later, as the attendees filed out the door, one elderly gentleman turned to another and remarked, "I didn't understand a word they said." Do you think he ever called them to find out?

It seems as though brokers inevitably talk over the heads of their clients and prospects. They speak in an arcane jargon trying to persuade people to open accounts. Sometimes they live with chart patterns, divergences, and crossovers so long that they forget there is another world out there, complete with another language. Sometimes they're simply trying to impress others with their expertise. It is difficult, of course, to take a highly technical subject and reduce it to everyday language. Yet, this is precisely what you must do if you hope to sell your program. You're selling to corporate executives, not floor traders or foreign exchange dealers.

Zig Ziglar, one of the most widely sought after motivational speakers in the nation, speaks on a seventh grade level. During his presentations, he limits his vocabulary to words of mostly one or two syllables. As he explains it, people may *converse* on a college level, but they *feel* on an elementary level. A presentation can be *felt* if it is delivered in simple, every day words. Take time to translate where necessary. Use analogies wherever possible. Use visual aids (overheads, slides, charts, etc.). Make them simple to understand. Stay with line diagrams and lots of white space. (Can you *really* understand those three-dimensional option charts?) If you are speaking conceptually and can get away with it, illustrate your examples in generic terms (FC instead of *Swiss francs*) and arbitrary values (100 instead of .86854). This way you avoid cluttering the listener's mind with yesterday's irrelevant values carried to lengthy decimal places. It also safeguards you against getting bogged down in the middle of a presentation if your math skills are less than stellar.

Chart Patterns and Tea Leaves

A further word about charts. Do not show charts plastered over with waves, wedges, triangles, etc. If you can avoid it, don't get into technical analysis at all; this can be a Pandora's box. If you start explaining the importance of the Fibonacci sequence in Elliot wave theory, for example, you could easily spend the rest of your time talking of nothing else. Even if your listeners understand it, will they buy it? The general public still needs meat-and-potato fundamentals. These are the things that make real sense, whether or not they make predictive sense. Technical analysis is too much like tea leaf reading-hardly the impression you want to create with an audience still struggling with the difference between futures markets and gaming tables.

Of course, if your hedge model is going to incorporate technical analysis as a means of predicting currency moves, you must disclose this fact to your audience. So disclose it and move on. You can get into specifics later. Remember, unless you first sell the concept, the details won't matter much.

"So You're Into Derivatives"

It used to be that the word *commodities* enveloped all one needed to know about trading, speculating, and hedging, but the term took on a negative connotation after the inflationary bubble of the late 1970s was punctured and trading profits were given back *en masse*. The public, for a time, had had its fill of commodities. So *futures* came along as a replacement. This word, in turn, was replaced with *derivatives,* to separate the up-and-coming risk-management industry from its more earthy and speculative roots. Now we can read about derivatives and bankruptcies every time we pick up a newspaper. So much for image building.

It is unfortunate, because it makes the task of presenting currency management much more difficult. Perhaps you have to separate plain vanilla forwards, futures and options from the more exotic over-the-counter derivatives and not move forward until your prospect can recite the difference. Perhaps you should simply avoid the term *derivatives* altogether. Instead, refer to a *contract,* an *option,* a *private party agreement,* a *deferred exchange,* etc. You certainly should not promote derivatives such as embedded option strategies unless you carefully dissect them in front of your listeners, identifying each component as a long or short provision or contract. The instrument then becomes much less intimidating. Make no mistake about it—futures and options are intimidating to corporate America. One CEO remarked about how his board, without a second thought, gives blanket approval for forward contracts worth hundreds of millions of dollars in raw materials, but balks at approving twenty futures contracts for British pounds because futures are too risky.

Hedge Vehicles Come Last

Development of a currency management program does not begin with the sale of the particular financial instrument; it begins with the sale of a foreign exchange survey. Then you develop programs, policy, and models based on the results. The selection of specific hedging vehicles lies near the end of the process. By following this approach, you don't have to deal with the negative connotations of derivatives until the principals of hedging are well understood and accepted. If you're a broker or dealer, your involvement implies that derivatives will play a part in the program. Leave it at that. The time to select exactly which hedge vehicles to use comes later. The credibility you've established with the company in the meantime can overcome any aversion to the use of these techniques. Of course, it may turn out that derivatives of any type just don't fit the situation or the risk profile of the company. It may turn to non-leveraged techniques such as bank borrowings instead. This is another reason why the survey should stand alone as a chargeable sales product. Then you won't spend all that time with a prospect without some form of compensation.

The Individual Buyer

So far, the discussion of selling has been very general. Principles that work in almost every presentation and with almost every listener have been presented; however, there is another dimension to selling currency risk management. Rather than considering the company as a whole, take stock of the individuals who make up the organization. Each has some say in the final decision of the company, for better or worse. Robert Miller and Stephen Heiman explore these influences at length in their best seller, *Strategic Selling*. Put this book on your "must read" list. Many of the concepts below were developed from their work.[1]

Every time you contact a prospect to sell, present, educate, or inform, you essentially are asking someone (a buyer) to do something (buy). This buyer then makes a decision on whether or not to do it. The decision to buy may be in the form of final approval of the program, acceptance of the team concept, acceptance of a survey, a commitment to set time aside to listen or to bring others into the meeting, or anything else that furthers the sales process. Regardless of what it is we are selling at the moment, we assume that the person we are selling to has the authority to buy. Otherwise, why would he or she take the time to talk with us, or show interest in what we say?

There are several dynamics to be aware of in a hierarchical organization such as a corporation. First, there is one, and only one, person in the organization with the authority to make a particular buying decision at a particular moment in time. This authority oftentimes is formally bestowed on an individual—it comes with the territory. The role of the purchasing agent is a good example. Many times, however, the buying power passes from hand to hand in a much more casual fashion. Whoever has the interest, the time, the expertise, or is in the mood may be the buyer of the moment. The second time you visit, someone else may be the buyer, even when you are restating the same proposal.

There are also times that buying authority passes from one individual to another on an *unconscious* level. This is the case, for example, when no one, either in or out of the company, knows for sure who has the last word on the matter until it is expressed. This often occurs in the heat of office politics involving power plays, turf battles, defensive maneuvering, and so on. When these dynamics are in play, the person who expresses so much interest in what you say may not be the buyer, even if he implies to you that he is. He may not want to reveal that he has lost the authority to buy. He may not even be aware of the fact.

This single-buyer dynamic comes into play whether you buttonhole one individual in the hallway, or address an entire group, such as an executive committee. During a group meeting, seven or eight individuals may fire blistering questions at you, make copious notes, nod or shake their heads. It's all show. Committees do not make buying decisions. There is only one person in the group who has that authority. Even when the decision is by consensus, this is the person who sways the vote. The position or title may identify this person, but not always; therefore, it is important to know for sure who the real buyer is before walking into a meeting. When you fail to identify him correctly, he will always turn out to be the person who was nodding off in the corner; the dummy you totally ignored.

The Personal Benefit

Identifying the buyer is the first step. Your challenge is to provide him with a win. Consultative selling, remember, requires that both buyer and seller walk away winners. What does it take for a buyer to win? A common assumption is that the buyer wins when the buyer's company wins. It is essential, after all, that the company benefit from your service. Almost every manager, every employee, wants to see his or her company remain healthy. Paychecks depend on it. Knowing this, your proposal may be based solely on what benefits the company, but this benefit is too abstract to be felt on an emotional level. Fundamental to successful selling is recognition of the fact that buyers buy (and win) *emotionally*.

This is certainly no revelation. The principle of emotional buying is bedrock to the advertising industry. It is why salespeople sell benefits, not features. An owner of a hardware store, for example, does not promote the growing attributes of grass seed and vegetable seed, although they may be impressive features. Rather, he sells green lawns and bountiful gardens. These are the benefits provided by the features. The presentation of currency management works in a similar fashion. Risk reduction is a feature, and certainly core to the whole concept of hedging, but the buyer wants to know why this feature is advantageous *to him*. He needs to personally benefit before he is interested.

This is not good news. You are not selling one product to one buyer. In the process of developing a currency management program, you are selling a number of products (concepts, really) on a number of occasions to a number of buyers. They all have different needs. A potential increase in corporate earnings, for example, may drive one buyer because it means an increased bonus. It may leave a second buyer who doesn't receive bonuses completely unmoved. This person, however, may strive for increased recognition or a reduction in stress. If you do no more than correctly identify each buyer who comes along, your chances of success certainly increase. If you also correctly identify what it is that each buyer needs to have to win, and can deliver that win, you have every chance of being outstanding in this business.

Miller and Heiman categorize potential buyers by function and by the personal benefits most commonly associated with that function. Look for these "buying influences" as you make your presentation. These are the *coach*, the *user buyer*, the *technical buyer*, and the *economic buyer*. Each of these influences may impact the program as you develop it. Each may be *the* buyer at a particular stage, the one you must win over before proceeding to the next step.

Do you really have to sell them all? Certainly, not all of these buying influences make the final decision. Only one can financially commit the company. This is probably the chief executive officer or a director. Why not bypass a particularly obstreperous individual whom you know has no final buying authority in this process? Why not make a beeline to the final buyer? Do so at your peril. While it is true that only one person is authorized to buy any particular proposal you present along the way, this is not the case in reverse. Any number of individuals might have the authority to *not* buy; that is, they may have the power to influence the final buyer not to buy. This is why they are called "buying influences." Most often, you will have no way of knowing who can influence what. The solution, then, is to cover all the bases. Find all buying influences that can impact your program, and sell each one on how he personally benefits from currency risk management.

Eight Prospecting Considerations

The broker who prospects corporate clients for currency management business must be prepared to devote a significant amount of time to this endeavor. The objective is a long-term business relationship, so the effort put forth can be very worthwhile. Review the following considerations and plan your prospecting program accordingly.

1. Selling a currency management program requires consultative selling, a technique for providing a win-win situation for both buyer and seller.

2. The potential financial impact of a proposed currency management program requires that the broker be both credible and knowledgeable.

3. Selling the program involves a number of stages and concepts; therefore, the sale should be viewed as a process occurring over time. It includes a series of presentations or proposals.

4. All else being equal, a less technical presentation is more effective than one that is more technical. In-depth discussions of derivatives should take place only after the general concepts of currency management have been accepted.

5. Only one person will be empowered to buy or not to buy a specific proposal on a specific occasion. A subsequent proposal may involve a different buyer. In each case, the buyer may or may not be readily identifiable.

6. Although there is only one buyer at a time, there may be a number of individuals who influence the buyer's decision; therefore, everyone impacted by the program should be sold on its merits.

7. Individuals buy because of a perceived personal benefit. They do not buy features. A personal benefit creates the "win" in a selling situation. The broker must try to identify both the buyer and the buyer's personal "win."

8. Corporate functions, those who fulfill them, and their associated "wins" can be classified as buying influences. These are called the *coach*, the *user buyer*, the *technical buyer*, and the *economic buyer*. These classifications include "real" buyers as well as individuals who can influence the buyer's decision.

The Coach

The first buying influence to identify is the *coach*. This individual may or may not have actual buying authority; however, he does exert a major influence on your chances of success with the company. The coach is unique because, more than anything else, he "buys" *you*. The coach benefits personally by your success. Perhaps he wants you to succeed because he knows the importance of managing foreign exchange exposure. He sees you as the solution, and wants the recognition of presenting you to management. Perhaps you and the prospective coach hit it off right away and he simply finds satisfaction in watching you prevail.

Often, but not always, the coach is your contact person; perhaps, the one you met during the initial visit. Your *first objective* when prospecting for a new account is to *find a coach*. This person will be invaluable as he guides you through the corporate politics, opening doors. He also will help you to identify other buyers and buying influences. As this title implies, the coach will actively support you, up to a point. He will not sell for you. The reason, beside the fact that he probably is not a salesman, is because he is sold on your capabilities to sell yourself and your product.

What do you offer to acquire someone's active support? Your credibility and knowledge. Unless a prospective coach finds you credible, he will not take a chance on you. Your coach, after all, may be risking his own reputation and credibility by promoting you. Who do you look for? Someone who can relate to your knowledge base; someone who already has a basic understanding of trading and risk management. You probably will find your coach in corporate finance. Try the treasurer first, then go from there.

The Technical Buyer

The *technical buyer* rarely has any real buying authority. He is a buyer, however, because of the influence he can exert on other buyers, including those with real authority. The technical buyer is the corporate "shopper." He may be a company employee, or an outside professional with an advisory or oversight function. This buyer, more than any other, sees himself as a guardian, protecting the corporation from products and salespeople who don't measure up. He plays the devil's advocate by kicking the tires.

Technical buyers *compare*. They study the merits of a product and compare them with competing products or alternative solutions. After talking to you, they may actually solicit your competitor to come in and make a proposal, just to give the company a choice in the matter. They screen out anyone who doesn't make the grade. Nothing is approved by management without their consent, or so they believe. When selling to someone whom you mistook for an authoritative buyer, more often than not it was a technical buyer. As far as this person is concerned, until you pass muster, he is the buyer. Purchasing agents fulfill this role very nicely. So do the following:

• The corporate attorney

• The corporate accountant

• The bank officer

• The securities broker

• The management consultant

• The financial consultant

Technical buyers are natural cynics. Financial consultants are good examples, especially when it concerns someone else's product. When asked for an opinion of a hedging program (other than his), he immediately guards the gates. He carefully scrutinizes the program for flaws, and unhesitatingly gives a thumbs down if he finds the least discrepancy. Although he cannot give approval for the company, he may have the power to *disapprove.* In either case, the personal benefit to the technical buyer is that he gets to display his expertise and protect a client by detecting faults that others might miss. The personal benefit to most technical buyers is recognition, or sometimes the power to say no. Achieving accolades by saving the company from a bad business decision can be very satisfying. So technical buyers look for problems.

Try to avoid these people unless they truly are significant to your success. If the CEO tells you to "run it past Dan," and Dan is the corporate tax attorney, you're going to be in for a bad day. If you must sell to an important technical buyer and it's going down hill, offer to make him a member of the currency management team (assuming you can deliver on the offer). As a team player, he will be recognized and his input and scrutiny could be of value. Make the offer over lunch and pick up the tab.

The User Buyer

A particular company may have any number of *user buyers.* These are the "hands on" people. He will be involved in the actual management of foreign currency. It's up to him to make the program work for his department, and for the company as a whole. He can also make it *not* work if he feels it was foisted upon him against his will. The user buyer, therefore, is more influential than any one else once the program is up and running because he is in charge of running it. When possible, every significant user buyer should be made a part of the currency management team, and should be involved in the development of the program at an early stage.

The treasurer will usually be the primary user buyer. (If you are fortunate, he will also be your coach.) Not all user buyers are found in the area of finance, however. Sales, marketing, and production have large stakes in how currency exposures affect the company's performance. The distinction between financial and non-financial user buyers involves the personal benefit each derives from your program. Whereas treasury will gain control over the currency (a definite "win"), the user buyers in operating functions may actually *lose* control. This is the case, for example, if margins and performance figures are now to be translated at exchange rates determined by treasury, rather than by happenstance.

This loss of control can turn a neutral user buyer into an active antagonist very quickly. Any hedge program forced upon a manager without his input, especially one which affects his area of operation, will be viewed by him as a threat. Look to counter this by personal "wins" in other areas. The head of a distribution unit may not be overly impressed by the fact that hedging can reduce risk on the corporate balance sheet, but what about the program's ability to gain a competitive edge on job quotes? A reduction in accounting exposure benefits finance. Reductions in operating exposure, and the subsequent potential boost in performance, benefits the operational buyer. Remember that the performance of this person is often measured by the variances in operating income. Make the non-financial user buyer a part of the team, or at least take the time to solicit his input. Address his concerns. Keep him informed. Remember- every one has to see how they win or the program will be short-lived, if it succeeds in getting off the ground.

The Economic Buyer

This is your most challenging buying influence. The final decision to commit the company to your proposals rests with the buyer who holds the purse strings. It is common knowledge in sales that the more impact the product or service has on the company, the higher up the ladder one must look for a final commitment to buy. Currency management, of course, can have a profound impact on the corporate net worth. The final authority for this type of program will rest with one of the directors or with one of the officers, probably the CEO. If no one on this level knows you, you have not yet sold the company. Sometimes, however, you find a person at a mid-management level has been given final buying authority. Beware. That usually means that those at the executive level have not heard of your program. When they do, you may have to resell it from the beginning.

Since the directors or corporate officers are the final decision-makers, you should become very familiar with the two officers most likely to be involved, the *chief executive officer* and the *chief financial officer*. Of course, the individuals acting in these capacities may have different titles. The treasurer or the director of finance may fulfill the CFO's function. The CEO may be the president, the executive director, the general manager, or the owner. Your concern is with a particular set of responsibilities more than the title, and with the type of person who rises to the top to accept these responsibilities.

The CFO Looks for Solutions

Rarely will currency management of any kind succeed without the active and ongoing support of the CFO. After all, the program will be under his direction; therefore, you need to be well aware of what the CFO requires in the way of personal benefits before he is interested in your product.

Think of the company as a sailing ship, plying the seas of commerce. The chief executive officer is the captain. With sextant and compass, he watches the stars. The chief financial officer (CFO), on the other hand, rarely concentrates on anything that distant. Rather, he focuses on the water line. It is his duty to keep the ship afloat. The CFO does not have time to sit and project the company's position in five or ten years. He is more interested in where it is *right now*. He views things with a weather eye, and is the first to notice an approaching stormy sea. Unlike the technical buyer, the CFO doesn't look for problems. He doesn't need to. They fill his calendar daily, and each requires his urgent attention daily. He continually seeks *solutions*, on a personal as well as a corporate level. Miller and Heiman write that a solution to a problem is the most powerful of all buying motivators.[2] When wallowing in heavy seas, nothing takes precedence over keeping the ship upright. Other personal benefits, such as opportunity, growth, and recognition, can wait.

This need of the CFO is very much to your advantage. Currency management is built around problem solving. It is, after all, the method by which financial risk is transferred away from the company. When this has been effectively communicated, the CFO often becomes one of the pro-gram's stauchest promoters, and a driving force for moving it forward.

When making your presentation to the CFO, go ahead and dwell on risk reduction. On the other hand, do not carry on at all about the profit potential. If you have a "profitable" trading system that "can make you money when traded right," the CFO is the very last person you want to talk to about it. This buyer wants to *reduce* risk, not increase it with new trading adventures, nor will he exhibit a lot of enthusiasm over the novel, the experimental, or the little-known approaches to currency manage-ment. All too risky. He wants hedging techniques that have been tested, proven, and preferably carved in stone from public usage. Don't mention the word *derivative* if you can help it; the CFO's favorite financial instru-ment is the U.S. treasury bill.

This buyer is not a risk taker; he is a financial engineer. He will show a great deal of interest in the details of future roll overs, bull strategies in option combos, and the like, including how and when funds and securi-ties are transferred, where accounts are located, who has custody, and so forth. He may understand these concepts at least as well as you do. Do your product homework thoroughly before meeting with the CFO. Remember that this person requires *security* and *stability*. Be prepared for questions concerning the financial strength of your firm and your length of employment. Promote this, if it is a strength. If it is not, emphasize the custodial regulations and clearing member's security of customer funds, regardless of the broker holding the account.

This buyer has a major interest in hedging *accounting* exposures, those in which the risk of exposure is most immediate and visible. If you are proposing a program that emphasizes the management of operating exposure at the *expense* of accounting exposure, give a lot forethought to how you will explain it to the CFO.

The CEO Looks for Opportunities

Let's meet the captain of the ship. Whereas the CFO keeps an eye on the structure, the CEO fixes his sight on the horizon. This buyer is a futurist, and the next five years are where he lives most of the time. This buyer possesses a great deal of imagination, required of a visionary. He is charged with knowing the changes in the industry before they happen, and with making course corrections accordingly. The CEO is akin to the farmer who looks over snow-covered fields and sees wheat ready for har-vest. Whether that occurs depends a great deal on his decisions and efforts. An unquenchable faith in one's self is a characteristic of both farmer and CEO. It is an essential ingredient in risk-taking and, if nothing else, the CEO is the quintessential risk taker. He tunes in to words such as *forward-looking, forewarned, strategic goals.* His personal wins include concepts such as *growth, opportunity,* and *success.* To achieve these, he always is seeking the high ground, the competitive advantage. The CEO has little patience with details; he can delegate those. He works almost totally with concepts.

Talk *strategically* to this buyer. There must be a competitive advantage to using your proposals. How does your program help penetrate new markets or expand existing ones? How does it help increase market share? If the chief financial officer wants a hedging system that is well-known and accepted, the CEO, on the other hand, is more interested in the system nobody knows about. Remember that this buyer, above all, is a competitor. He looks for the inside edge.

There are other distinctions between these two buyers. The CFO focuses on accounting exposures. The CEO often is more concerned with long-term operating exposures, rather than quarter-to-quarter changes in the balance sheet. In your presentation to the CEO, think about how your concept or recommendations create product differentiation, new avenues of sourcing, the ability to bid or price in local currency. The CEO strives to enhance profitability. Your presentation should illustrate how currency management does just that.

The major difference between these two buyers involves the matter of risk. Whereas the CFO is risk averse, the CEO is a gambler. If we begin to emphasize the speculative profit potential of our hedge strategy, the CFO quickly finds that he is late for another appointment. The CEO is more likely to extend the time of our meeting in order to learn the details. Knowing this, a derivative salesman might enhance the speculative aspects of a hedging program to get it past the CEO. This, of course, is unethical and quite possibly damaging to the client. The consequences may include future litigation. If there are speculative elements in your program, such as a selective hedging model, make absolutely sure that no unrealistic expectations are generated.

The CEO's decision is ultimately the one that counts, so your presentation to him is a make-or-break situation. Because you want all bases covered before approaching him, he often is the last on your list. Not always. Sometimes it is the CEO who is the most interested in currency management. He may even initiate the first contact, leaving it to you to sell others in the organization. The most important point to remember is that, no matter where you start, you must meet individuals, talk with them, and come away with everyone a winner. See Figure 7-1 for a summary of the presentation process.

Figure 7-1: The Presentation Process

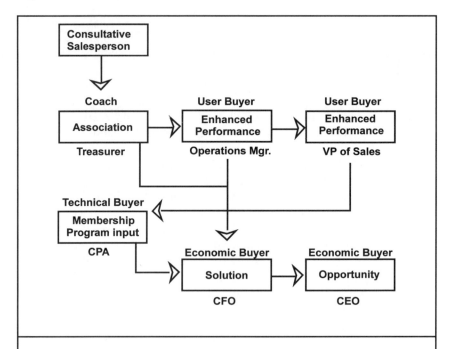

This diagram illustrates a possible presentation process for a currency management program. The consultative salesperson looks for the personal benefit
for each buyer he encounters in order to effect a win-win situation. He or she
first identifies a coach, someone who wins because the salesperson wins. This
may be the treasurer, the financial manager, or someone acting in that capacity. The personal benefits, or "wins," are shown here within the boxes desig-
nating the various buyer positions and influences. The process culminates
with a final presentation to the CEO.

The presentation is not always "uphill." The arrows often point the other
way. Sometimes the CEO or CFO will start the process by finding sources to
handle their exposures. The company may then be calling you.

A Final Word

Corporate risk management can only continue to grow along with a free market economy. Within this field, perhaps nothing is more challenging than the management of foreign exchange. Foreign currencies offer a little of everything—volatile markets, speculative interest, political intrigue, international finance, and sometimes high drama. Foreign currencies are certainly in the public eye much more than pork bellies or oats.

As a futures broker, foreign currency hedging comprised a significant portion of my business. A number of concepts found in this book were developed by trial and error, as I prospected and serviced these accounts. I was one of a partnership of two. I did not trade as well as my partner, who seemed to have a knack for it. That worked out fine for me because I enjoyed getting out and prospecting. Walking through a door the first time into who knows what can be a rather heady experience.

The information, techniques, and suggestions offered in this handbook take time to digest. Selling one's way through a major corporation, from one office to the next, can be daunting. Fortunately, this process almost never goes strictly "by the book." In fact, if the truth be known, I cannot think of a single major account in our partnership which came about because I initiated the first contact. (On the other hand, I can think of a great many prospecting calls that went nowhere.) Virtually every one of our major accounts was opened by an individual, corporate or otherwise, who walked in out of the blue and cornered me in my office when I wasn't looking.

I became a firm believer in psychic power. Many times our business slowed to an absolute crawl. My partner and I would sit, our eyes fixated on the monitor screen, fighting off black cord disease. (That's where you pick up the phone and would just as soon wrap the cord around your neck as to actually use it to call a prospect.) Eventually, someone would remark that perhaps we should consider opening our book to new clients. I would commit to becoming a salesman again.

And that's when the phone would begin to ring. Prospects we had never heard of called in to check on bond prices, or corn, or TED spreads. A few would call in to see what we knew about hedging, including hedging currencies.

I began to realize that success in opening accounts is not derived from *following* a prospecting plan as much as simply *having* one; but to be successful, you must be totally committed to the one you have. This may seem contradictory at first, but it is a true statement. You can build a thriving business in currency risk management without following all of the recommendations in this book. In fact, you can be very successful without doing a single thing we've outlined, but you must be completely *willing* to do *everything* this book suggests, down to the last step.

It is not what you do as much as what you are ready and willing to do. You must continuously be prepared to make every presentation, talk to every prospect, put on every seminar. Perhaps the account opens only after you do it all. Perhaps it opens before you even start. Probably it will be somewhere in between. Remember, the secret is not in *doing*. It is in the *willingness* to do.

This, by the way, is not an original technique. I first came across it in a Nightingale-Conant audio program by Mike Hernacki, entitled, "The Ultimate Secret to Getting Absolutely Everything You Want!" Try it. In some mystical fashion, it works.

Being willing means being prepared. Stay on top of the currency markets. Learn about the local industry. Identify the companies in your area that export or import. Discover who the officers are. Develop a foreign exchange survey and test it, hypothetically if you must. Make calls. Write letters. Somehow, the knowledge that you are the expert in foreign currency gets around faster than you can. Don't worry about finding the right prospect. The right prospect will find you.

Good luck, and good fortune.

Appendix I
Topic Review

Chapter One

I.   Which of the following companies have foreign currency exposure?

    1.   A U.S. manufacturer who sells products overseas and denominates its price sheets in the foreign currency;

    2.   A U.S. service provider who contracts internationally and invoices solely in U.S. dollars;

    3.   A distributor in the United States which restricts its sales to the domestic market. It procures inventory abroad which results in foreign currency payables

    4.   A U.S. producer that markets only domestically. Although it sources internationally, it accepts invoices from foreign vendors denominated only in U.S. dollars.

        1 only
        1 & 3
        1, 2 & 3
        1, 2, 3 & 4

II.   Laker Air was subjected to the following types of exposure.

    1.   Cash flow

    2.   Accounting

    3.   Operating

    4.   Strategic

1 & 2
2 & 3
3& 4
All of the above

III.   Name three methods of hedging

1. _____

2. _____

3. _____

IV.   Transaction hedging is the most effective means to manage:

1. Accounting exposure
2. Cash flow exposure
3. Operating exposure
4. Strategic exposure

1 & 2
2 & 3
3 & 4
All of the above

V.   Foreign currency management is more important now than in the past because of:

1. An increasing number of pegged currencies
2. An increasing volatility in currency markets
3. An increasing number of foreign exchange transactions
4. The increasing stature of the U.S. dollar

1
1 & 2
2 & 3
2 & 4

VI.   In general, foreign currency exposure means that there is a
      _____ in some aspect of the operation.

Answers to Chapter One

I. (1, 2, 3 & 4) 1 and 3 are perhaps the most obvious examples of exposure. Any change in the rate of exchange between the dollar and the foreign currency would impact revenues or receivables (1), and the liabilities on the balance sheet (3). Not as obvious are (2) and (4), which are examples of hidden exposure. (2) has exposure in all its overseas markets. It may be priced out of these markets if the dollar strengthens. (4) can be adversely affected two ways by foreign currency exposure: if the currency of the vendor increases

in value relative to the dollar, the vendor may increase the dollar price or discontinue supplying the producer.

II. (all of the above) Laker Air's revenue, or cash flow, was dependent on the British pound remaining strong relative to the U.S. dollar, since the relatively low value of the dollar enticed British vacationers to travel to New York. In addition, Laker Air contracted accounting exposure in the same direction by entering into major long-term purchasing agreements denominated in U.S. dollars.

Operating exposure involves the company's competitive position. Laker Air's operation revolved around the perception of New York as an economical vacation spot, a perception that changed with the exchange rate. Because the company's entire business consisted solely of flying "bargain hunting" British vacationers to New York, it is apparent that the exposure was strategic in nature. Actually, Laker Air was exposed to a single risk—the variability of the dollar/pound exchange rate. This example illustrates that the differences between exposures are largely a matter of perspective.

III. Operating strategies, financial adjustments, and transactional hedging.

IV. (1 & 2) The contractual nature of accounting exposure makes it an ideal candidate for management by transactional hedging, which is also contractual in nature. Noncontractual items of cash flow can sometimes be effectively hedged with market transactions that have conditional features, such as option strategies, if the anticipated exposure values can be determined.

V.   (2 & 3) There is sufficient evidence that the tremendous increase in
        the volume of currency trading has, in part, produced much greater
        volatility, which, in turn, makes the risk of exposure too pro-
        nounced to leave unmanaged.

VI.   (Currency mismatch). This is most visible on the balance sheet,
        where it produces accounting exposure.

Chapter Two

I. One fast-growing market for foreign currency management that is most accessible is:

    1. Multinational companies
    2. Municipalities
    3. The retail industry
    4. Mid-sized corporations

II. The currency markets include:

    1. The cash market
    2. The interbank network
    3. The futures exchanges
    4. The over-the-counter market

       1 & 2
       2 & 3
       1, 2 & 3
       1, 2, 3 & 4

III. In dollar value, how much foreign exchange is transacted globally in the currency markets daily?

    1. $10 million
    2. $50 billion
    3. $1 trillion
    4. $10 trillion

IV. What percentage of the above transactions takes place in the interbank?

    1. 8%
    2. 32%
    3. 51%
    4. 96%

V.   A "17 bid ask 21" quote in Deutsche marks means:

   1.   I buy DM at 17 and sell at 21
   2.   I buy dollars at 17 and sell at 21
   3.   I buy DM at 21 and sell at 17
   4.   I buy dollars at 21 and sell at 17

VI. Of the following British pound exchange rates, which are direct
     quotes and which are indirect quotes?

   1.   1.5600
   2.   .6578
   3.   .6632
   4.   1.5202

VII. Which two are reciprocals of each other?

   1.   1.5600
   2.   .6578
   3.   .6632
   4.   1.5202

VIII. Assume that the DM is trading at .57787 and SF at .68658. What
     is the DM/SF cross rate?

   1.   1.1881
   2.   1.2290
   3.   .8416
   4.   .3968

IX. The best description of a spot/forward swap is:

   1.   Taking delivery of spot and selling it forward
   2.   Buying spot and selling forward
   3.   Rolling spot forward
   4.   Selling spot and buying forward

1 & 4
1 & 2
3
2 & 4

X. Foreign exchange dealers are normally compensated by:

1. An undisclosed flat fee

2. A commission on the spread

3. A profit on the trade

4. The spread between the bid and the offer

XI. Forward positions can be liquidated by:

1. Offset ahead of the value date

2. Delivery when value date becomes spot

3. Neither of the above

4. Both of the above

XII. The broker has a competitive edge over the foreign exchange dealer in the following areas:

1. Regulatory oversight

2. Credit risk

3. Transaction cost

4. Value date settlement

1 & 2
2 & 3
1, 2 & 3
2, 3 & 4

Answers to Chapter Two

I.   (4) Although all enterprises that conduct international business are prospects for foreign currency management, the mid-sized corporation (with $15 to $100 million annual sales) is the most accessible. These companies most often use local or regional banks instead of the major banks. Also, the decision makers are more accessible than those in larger companies. Equally important to brokers and dealers with access to the exchange, futures transaction costs can compare very favorably to the interbank, and contracts are closer in size to average exposures of mid-sized corporations. Of course, the exposure for any prospect must be in an exchange-traded currency, or a close proxy thereof.

II.   (1, 2, 3, & 4) The interbank is by far the largest market. The others engage more in trading derivatives of the underlying interbank spot values. Currency options also trade both over-the-counter and on various futures, stock, and options exchanges.

III. (3) Approximately one trillion dollars is exchanged daily. This is the *notional* value (the size of the contract) rather than actual outlay.

IV.   (4) The other markets are minute, compared to the interbank business.Still, they account for approximately $40 billion worth of foreign exchange every trading day.

V.   (2) The interbank convention is to buy and sell U.S. dollars for other currencies. "17" and "21" are indirect quotes, with the lower value translating into more dollars per foreign currency unit and vice versa; therefore, the dealer buys more dollars at 17 and pays out fewer dollars at 21.

VI.   1 and 4 are direct quotes, referring to the number of dollars in one pound. Indirect quotes refer to the number of foreign currency units in one dollar. Note: the interbank uses indirect quotes except for certain British commonwealth currencies, such as the British pound, the Irish punt, and the Australian dollar, which are quoted *directly in all markets.*

VII. (2 and 4) Direct and indirect quotes of a given rate of exchange are reciprocals. The reciprocal of any number can be found by dividing 1.00 by that number. For example, 1.00/.6578 equals 1.5202 (rounded). Also, one reciprocal multiplied by the other always equals 1.00.

VIII. (1) We are looking for the cross rate of DM/SF, or the number of Deutsche marks in one Swiss franc. (The ratio, "SF/DM," on the other hand, refers to the number of Swiss francs in one Deutsche mark.)To find any "x/y" cross rate, multiply the *indirect* quote for "x" by the *direct* quote for "y." The direct quote for DM is given as .57787, so the indirect quote is 1.7305 (1 /.57787). The direct quote for the SF is given at .68658; therefore, 1.7305 x .68658 equals 1.1881.

IX. (2 & 4) A swap is identical in configuration to a futures calendar spread, in which one month is bought and the other month is sold. "Tomorrow/next" swaps can be viewed as "one day-two day" spreads; "spot/next" swaps as "two day–three day" spreads, "spot/forward" swaps as "two day–more than two day" spreads, and forward/ forward swaps as "more than two day–more than two day" spreads. There is an exception to these comparisons. The spot CD/$ rate is a one day, not a two day, forward rate.

X. (4) Foreign exchange dealers operate as principals who buy and sell at different prices when dealing with customers and other dealers.

XI. (2) Forwards, unlike futures, can only be *liquidated* by delivery or offset on their value date, when they become spot. They can be *offset* ahead of the value date to lock in a gain or loss, but they are not *liquidated*. Rather, the positions continue to be marked to the market, generating offsetting gains and losses, until the value date.

XII. (1, 2 & 3) Answer #4, "value date settlement," offers a competitive advantage for the use of forwards, which can be easily delivered, offset, or rolled forward at the option of the holder. The futures exchanges are not geared toward delivery (or receipt), and making or taking delivery is often discouraged by brokerage firms.

Chapter Three

I.   The three types of currencies are:

   1._____
   2._____
   3._____

II.   With regard to value, a fiat currency is:

   1.   Only as valuable as its redemption price
   2.   Intrinsically worthless
   3.   Worth only the value of the paper it's printed on
   4.   Worth-dependent upon the rate of interest

III.   The exchange rate regime of the major foreign currencies is considered to be:

   1.   A single currency peg
   2.   A cooperative arrangement
   3.   A floating system of some sort
   4.   Pegged primarily to the inflation index of the country

IV.   A government might restrict the convertibility of its currency by using: (select all that apply)

1.   A multiple market system
2.   A parallel market system
3.   Excessive spreads
4.   Selected taxes and subsidies

V.   The PPP theory states that purchasing power parity between currencies is maintained primarily by:

1.   Cooperative purchasing arrangements
2.   Arbitrage

3. Intervention

4. The relative anticipated depreciation of each currency

VI. The real rate of exchange varies:

    1. In direct proportion to the nominal rate of exchange

    2. In indirect proportion to the nominal rate of exchange

    3. Independently of the spot rate

    4. Independently of the nominal rate

VII. Assume that in January, the FC/HC rate was trading at 1.00. Six months later, it was trading at 1.10. Prices in both countries remained unchanged. We know that: (select all that apply)

    1. There was a change in the nominal rate of exchange

    2. There was no change in the nominal rate of exchange

    3. There was a change in the real rate of exchange

    4. There was no change in the real rate of exchange

VIII. Assume that a company contracts a one-year receivable denominated in the foreign currency FC. The FC Eurorate equals LIBOR less 1%. If the company hedges with a one-year futures contract:

    1. It will buy futures at a premium to spot

    2. It will buy futures at a discount to spot

    3. It will sell futures at a premium to spot

    4. It will sell futures at a discount to spot

IX. The following statements concerning interest rate parity are true: (select all that apply)

    1. The difference between spot and forward rates depends on the Eurorate differential

    2. Higher FC interest rates will increase the value of FC forwards over spot

    3. The difference between spot and forward is based on nominal interest rates

    4. The difference between spot and forward is based on real interest rates

X.   A foreign central bank suddenly drops its discount rate. Concerning the currency of the country, we know: (select all that apply)

    1. The impact on the forward exchange rate is greater than the impact on spot
    2. The spot rate moves more than the forward rate
    3. The forward rate increases relative to spot
    4. The forward rate may either increase, decrease, or stay the same

Answers to Chapter Three

I.   The three types of currencies are (1) *specie*, which are commonly struck as coins from precious metals, (2) *commodity-backed*, which are redeemable upon demand for a commodity such as gold or silver, and (3) *fiat*, which is unbacked.

II. (2) Fiat currency is intrinsically worthless and considered to be price indeterminable, which means that its only value is what the market quotes (in terms of another fiat currency) from one moment to the next. As paper currency, it has no intrinsic worth because it cannot be redeemed for anything of value. It is currency only because the people have grown accustomed to it.

III. (3) Either a managed or an independently floating system. Freely traded currencies may be value-determined in any of the IMF designated regimes from the inflexible single-currency pegs to the most flexible floating regimes. Key currencies and exchange-traded currencies all float, with rates determined by the market. Governments often "manage" the float through intervention or interest rate changes.

IV. (1, 3 and 4) Governments may use any of these methods for restricting the exchange rate or convertibility of its currency. Another practice, according to the IMF, is to fix the exchange rate for certain transactions. A "parallel market" is a euphemism for "black market," and almost never government sanctioned.

V.   (2) Arbitrage. Purchasing power parity occurs when there is free movement of goods and services across boarders so competitive forces can bring prices (including currency prices) into parity with each other. Parity is achieved when profit-making opportunities based on a disparity of currency values no longer exist.

VI. (4) Real exchange rates, which are based on the relative purchasing power of currencies, rise and fall independently of the nominal rate. The relative value of nominal versus real rates changes daily, resulting in a price disparity that may last for years. ("Spot" can refer to either nominal or real rates.)

VII.   (1 and 3) There is a nominal change in rates of exchange. The nominal rate is the quoted market rate, which increased approximately 10%. The real rate also changed by the same amount because the relative inflation rate did not adjust to compensate for the nominal rate change.

VIII. (3) The company hedges by selling futures because the receivable represents an asset exposure. The FC pays 1% less than Eurodollar deposits. Because a lower-yielding currency is a premium currency, the company sells the one-year futures at a premium to spot.

IX.   (1 & 3) The price variance between spot and forward is an expression of the difference in Eurorates. Remember that the quoted price, whether pertaining to interest yield or foreign exchange, is always a nominal value. (The real rate must be calculated by factoring in the rate(s) of inflation.) Number (2) is false because a higher interest rate translates into a forward-rate discount.

X.   (3 & 4) All we can determine from the drop in interest rates is that the forward rates will increase in value over spot. This is based on the consequential decrease in the Eurorate relative to LIBOR. From the information given, we have no idea how the central bank action will affect the spot rate, or whether the impact on spot will be more or less than the impact on the forward. Spot may move more or less than the forward rates, depending on whether it goes up or down. The resulting move in forward rates, *in dollar value*, is completely dependent on where the spot rate ends up.

Chapter Four

I.   Examples of long and short positions might be:

    1.   Assets and liabilities
    2.   Production costs and sales receipts
    3.   Positions of equal value
    4.   All of the above

II.   An account depicts foreign exchange exposure if:

    1.   The account shows a mismatch of currencies
    2.   Both long and short positions are included in the account
    3.   There are open positions with future value dates
    4.   Account items are denominated in different currencies

III. Complete the following statement.

A hedge is the _____ of a given position by a position of _____, in which the effect of the offset _____ the effect of a change in values of both.

IV.   Assume that "Big and Best," a U.S. office supply company, imports a line of paper products from Canada. It reduces foreign exchange exposure of these imports by establishing a retail outlet in Vancouver. This is an example of transferring risk to the:

    1.   Supplier
    2.   Customer
    3.   Market place
    4.   Hedger

V.   Complete the following statement.

When a U.S. supplier sends its U.S. dollar-denominated price sheet to its overseas accounts, it is, in effect, exchanging _____ exposure for _____ exposure.

VI.   When an item is valued by one market at a price that correlates significantly with the price of another item in another market, the two markets are:

1.   Converging
2.   Convertible
3.   Parallel
4.   Establishing a basis

VII. Hedges should be placed in markets that have correlation coefficients no less than:

1.   50%
2.   70%
3.   80%
4.   100%

VIII. Compared to most commodity markets, arbitraging the currency markets is usually a very low cost, low risk undertaking because:

1.   The markets move in parallel
2.   The markets provide good spreading opportunities
3.   The markets are highly liquid
4.   The value by conversion is assured

IX.   Basis can be defined as:

1.   The price difference between two markets
2.   The correlation between two markets
3.   The convertibility between two markets
4.   The amount of gain or loss on the hedge position

X.   Complete the following statement:

Any two transactions that are denominated in a single currency and which together effectively offset foreign exchange exposure are _____ transactions.

Answers to Chapter Four

I. (4) All of the selections are examples of long and short positions. A "long" is defined as anything that benefits the holder by an increase in value. A "short" is defined as anything that benefits the holder by a decrease in value. Conversely, a decrease in value of a long or an increase in value of a short adversely affects the holder.

II. (1) Foreign exchange exposure exists only when there is a mismatch of currencies. This occurs when the sum of long positions in one currency does not equal in value the sum of short positions in the same currency.

III. A hedge is the *offset* of a given position by a position of *equal size* and *opposite direction.* The effect of the offsetting position is to *reduce or eliminate* the effects of changes in the value of both positions. Remember that, in general, an exposed position is *offset* when the long and short positions are in different markets, but *canceled* when the two positions are in the same market.

IV. (3) Market place. We can surmise that the company is paying for the imports in Canadian dollars because it has foreign exchange exposure. The retail outlet must transact in the local currency to obtain Canadian dollar receipts and offset the short position; thus, the risk is transferred to the market place rather than to the customer or supplier.

V. When a U.S. supplier sends its U.S. dollar-denominated price sheet to its overseas accounts, it is exchanging *accounting* exposure for *operating* exposure. It does this by transferring the risk to its customers, thereby jeopardizing its marketing position. It is also correct to say that the company is exchanging *visible* exposure for *hidden* exposure.

VI. (3) Parallel. The key to a parallel market is "significant correlation."

VII. (2) 70%. There is no magic coefficient that serves as a cut off point for hedge transactions. Some hedgers will not enter a market that has less than an 80% correlation. Basis risk is usually unacceptable under 70%. Basis risk is usually very low in currency transactional hedges because the two markets are valued identically.

VIII. (4) The value by conversion is assured. The "plain vanilla" currency derivatives, futures, options, and forwards settle for the same spot currency that produces the exposure. The assurance that the prices will converge produces a very low basis risk—or arbitrage risk, for that matter. This is not the case in many commodity futures, in which storage, grade, and location are all unknown cost factors at the time of delivery.

IX. (1) The basis can be defined as the price difference between two markets. The markets may be completely unrelated; the term "basis" does not necessarily imply price correlation.

X. Any two transactions that are denominated in a single currency, and which together effectively offset foreign exchange exposure, are *parallel market* transactions. This is a logical definition that allows the concepts and definitions of hedging to be applied to all three types of exposure management techniques: transactional, financial adjustments, and operating strategies.

Chapter Five

I.   The primary risk of operating exposure is its effect on:

   1. Assets and liabilities
   2. Cash receivables and payables
   3. Market share
   4. Plant and equipment

II.   Operating exposure (mark all that apply):

   1. Bears no necessary relationship to accounting exposure
   2. Pertains to nominal rather than real rates of exchange
   3. Is not necessarily associated with the currency in which prices are quoted
   4. Is not necessarily associated with the country in which products are sold or inputs sourced

III. The management of operating exposure must take into account both the nature of the company and its:

   1. Earnings
   2. Competition
   3. Balance sheet figures
   4. Nonfunctional currency transactions

IV.   Match the following techniques for suitability with *operating exposure, cash flow exposure,* or *accounting exposure.*

   1. Product modifications
   2. Short-term borrowing
   3. Roll-over (futures or forwards)
   4. Sourcing flexibility

V.   The two major types of accounting exposure are:

   1. _____
   2. _____

VI. Accounting exposures can be managed by hedging vehicles that have "like characteristics" such as:

    1. Contractual nature

    2. Same or similar currency

    3. Known value

    4. All of the above

VII. Foreign exchange gains and losses resulting from *nonfunctional* currency transactions are reported:

    1. On the income statement

    2. In the shareholder's equity section

    3. In the letter to the shareholders

    4. On the consolidated balance sheet

VIII. Foreign exchange gains and losses resulting from *functional* currency transactions are reported:

    1. On the income statement

    2. In the shareholder's equity section

    3. In the letter to the shareholders

    4. On the consolidated balance sheet

IX. Of the two types of accounting exposure, which is the most visible? Why?

    _____

    _____

X. Complete the following statement:

    The basic principle of positions of equal _____ and opposite _____ underlies all hedging, regardless of which technique is applied.

XI. Hedge accounting practices are important from the standpoint of:

1. Financial reporting
2. Cost of interest
3. Tax treatment
4. Currency swap agreements

XII. FASB 52 defines the type of hedge vehicle most suitable for:

1. Operating exposure
2. Transactional exposure
3. Cash flow exposure
4. Consolidated exposure

XIII. Cash flow exposure primarily affects the corporate:

1. Operating variance
2. Competitive position
3. Current assets and liabilities
4. Price/earnings ratio

XIV. Long-term fixed-rate borrowing is often a suitable management technique for both _____ exposure and _____exposure.

XV. Long-term (multi-year) borrowing from a bank for hedging purposes can be most effectively simulated by:

1. Forward exchange swaps
2. Futures calendar spreads
3. Currency swaps
4. Spot/forward roll-overs

XVI. "Leading and Lagging" refers to:

    1.   Contracting through letters of credit

    2.   Receivables and payables

    3.   The trade finance package

    4.   The product mix

Answers to Chapter Five

I.   (3) Market share. Operating exposure refers to the effects of exchange rate changes on the competitive position of the company, as well as on the capacity of its customers to purchase the product or the service.

II. (1, 3 and 4) Also, operating exposure is determined by the structure of the markets in which the company and its competitors source inputs and sell products. Note that this exposure produces profits and losses from real, not nominal, exchange rate changes. Changes in real exchange rates impact the purchasing power of the currency. This has a direct bearing on the customer's capacity to purchase as well as the company's capacity to source.

III. (2) Competition. The other choices concern items impacted by accounting exposure.

IV. Product modifications and sourcing flexibility are operating strategies used to manage operating exposure. Short-term borrowing is often used to hedge accounting exposure. Roll-overs, either with futures or forwards, could be considered for accounting exposure, cash flow exposure, or both. With either exposure type, roll-over techniques imply long-term exposure management.

V.   *Transactional* and *translation* exposures are the two major forms of accounting exposure. The difference, according to FASB 52, depends on whether the currency producing the exposure is a functional or a nonfunctional currency. Accounting exposure is sometimes referred to as balance sheet exposure or, when foreign operations are involved, consolidated after-tax exposure.

VI. (4) All of these elements are like characteristics. Accepted accounting definitions must also be taken into consideration. FASB 52 identifies a bona fide hedge for accounting purposes as one that (a) offsets an identifiable foreign currency commitment, (b) is designated as, and effective as, a hedge, and (c) must be a firm commitment in its own right.

VII. (1) Nonfunctional foreign currency transactions are those conducted by a company in a currency other than its own. Foreign exchange losses and gains from these transactions flow through to the income statement. This is known as "transactional exposure."

VIII. (2) Functional currency transactions are conducted in the company's own currency. They only produce an accounting exposure when they are reported on the parent company's balance sheet denominated in a different currency. The resulting translation gains and losses appear in the shareholder equity section of the balance sheet and are considered to be translation exposure.

IX. Tranactional exposure is the most visible because it affects the company's earnings and therefore has tax implications.

X. The basic principle of positions of equal size and opposite direction underlies all hedging, regardless of which technique is applied. We should add that this holds true whether or not operating, cash flow, or accounting exposure is being managed.

XI. (3) Hedge accounting, in practice, refers to deferred accounting. The idea is to defer tax reporting of hedge results until the foreign exchange gain or loss on the exposure is realized. The two items are then netted against each other to match up tax credits and debits.

XII. (2) Transactional exposure. See also answer 6 above. FASB 52 only addresses accounting exposure, which includes both transactional and translation exposures.

XIII. (1) Operating variance. Cash flow exposure is dynamic, unlike the static "snap shot" values produced by accounting exposure. The gains and losses caused by cash flow exposure can be identified by comparing the operating income from one period to another, and highlighting the variances due to exchange rate fluctuations. This process is known as variance analysis.

XIV. Long-term fixed-rate borrowing can be a suitable management technique for both *accounting* exposure and *cash flow* exposure. The currency borrowed must be exchanged for the home currency to "lock in" the exchange rate. Otherwise, the technique simply increases both liability and asset exposure.

XV. (3) Currency swaps. These counterparty agreements have the same effect as long-term bank borrowing. They are used primarily to take advantage of the counterparty's higher credit rating (and lower borrowing costs) in the local capital market.

XVI. (2) Receivables and payables. This is a financial adjustment to cash flow exposure in which stronger-currency receivables are held longer to take advantage of the upward trend, and weaker-currency receivables are collected quickly to limit market risk. The reverse procedure applies to the treatment of payables.

Chapter Six

I. The most effective way to manage foreign currency is from a:

    1. Strategic level
    2. Transaction level
    3. Operating level
    4. Translation level

II. A currency management program must take the following into consideration (list all that apply):

    1. The company
    2. The exposures
    3. The broker or banker
    4. The management team

III. A foreign exchange survey analyzes (list all that apply):

    1. The hedge model
    2. The competition
    3. The company's risk profile
    4. The currencies denominating assets and liabilities

IV. In regard to a foreign exchange survey, which of the following does not apply?

    1. It must be of perceived value to the client or prospect
    2. It should have no strings attached
    3. It should be limited to the types of exposures that you can effectively hedge
    4. It must compensate you for your effort

V. A survey questionnaire is used to:

    1. Select management team members
    2. Select the proper hedge model

3. Develop a hedging policy

4. Gather pertinent data for findings and recommendations

VI. The findings of a foreign exchange survey require that currency volatility be:

1. Predictable

2. Quantified

3. Qualified

4. Offset

VII. Which of the following is *not* a good reason to charge for the foreign exchange survey?

1. The survey should be highly profitable to the survey provider

2. The survey should represent value to the client

3. The survey should be free of conflict of interest for the survey provider

4. The time and effort expended requires compensation

VIII. Members of the currency management team might include:

1. The treasurer

2. Senior management

3. The Consultant or Advisor

4. All of the above

IX. Hedging often produces hedge losses. Explain why this is a reason to create a management team.

_____

_____

X. Beside transaction services, the most important contribution of the advisor on a corporate management team is:

1. Oversight

2. Education

3. Hedge Accounting

4. Market forecasts

XI. List four things to consider when developing an information management system:

1. _____

2. _____

3. _____

4. _____

XII. A basic requirement of any information management system is to:

1. Develop selective hedge models

2. Obtain an outside data vendor

3. Obtain real time quotes

4. Match hedges with exposed positions

XIII. Corporate hedging policy requires that a currency management program meet certain qualifications. These include:

1. Consistency with corporate objectives

2. Adherence to acceptable risk parameters

3. Transparency

4. All of the above

XIV. One important objective of a hedge model is to:

1. Plan a course of action beforehand

2. Insure that the hedge complies with corporate objectives

3. Provide assurances that no unwarranted risk is being taken

4. All of the above

XV. A company sells on a very thin margin, and creates foreign currency receivables. Management has little tolerance for foreign exchange loss. An appropriate currency management program could incorporate a:

   1. Range hedge model
   2. Classic 100% hedge model
   3. Trend-following model
   4. Option strategy

XVI. A company feels that its currency management team should be profitable. It is willing to tolerate a fairly high degree of market risk. The *least* appropriate hedge model for this objective is a:

   1. Range model
   2. Classic 100% hedge model
   3. Trend-following model
   4. Option strategy

XVII. Corporate policy should ensure that currency management is transparent. This means that:

   1. Only hedge positions that can be quickly liquidated should be considered
   2. "Plain vanilla" hedge strategies should be utilized
   3. Every aspect of the program is fully disclosed and understood
   4. All of the above

XVIII.From the standpoint of cost/benefit analysis, a viable currency management program must be:

   1. Profitable
   2. Structured so that gains and losses completely offset each other
   3. Not subjected to excessive transaction costs
   4. In compliance with standard hedge accounting rules

XIX. One of the most common and costly of all risks to consider in a stress test is:

   1. Liquidity Risk
   2. Operations Risk

3. Political Risk
4. Market Risk

XX. A currency swap suddenly produces losses because the counterparty is unable to meet its financial obligations. This is an example of:

1. Market Risk
2. Settlement Risk
3. Transfer Risk
4. Credit Risk

XXI. Which of the following trading rules should be incorporated in a hedging policy manual? (List those that apply)

1. Do not over-leverage
2. Always follow the trend
3. Update price charts daily
4. Do not liquidate simply to cut a loss

Answers to Chapter Six

I. (1) Strategic level. This refers to the measurement of all exposures as an aggregate. One exposure can impact another, either by augmenting or offsetting it. For this reason, management should commence from a strategic perspective which considers the overall risk.

II. (1) The company, (2) the exposures, and (4) the management team. Other considerations are the development of an information management system and a written policy concerning hedging. Although a knowledgeable broker or dealer can be a valuable team member, the program definitely should not be built around a particular transaction service or product. These can be considered at a later stage.

III. (2), (3) & (4). The competition, tolerance of risk, and the currencies creating exposure should all be considered in a foreign exchange survey. Selection of a hedge model comes later and is based on the findings of the survey.

IV. (3) A foreign exchange survey is a stand-alone product that should provide value to the company. To achieve this, all types of exposures must be analyzed because they are interrelated. Disregarding all exposures except those that the survey provider can hedge greatly diminishes the value of the survey.

V. (4) The questionnaire is used to gather pertinent data for findings and recommendations. The selection of a management team, hedge model, and the development of corporate policy should be based upon the results of the survey itself.

VI. (2) Quantified. The measurement of risk must factor in specific values. These values include volatility and dollar amount of the currencies producing the exposures.

VII. (1) The purpose of the survey is not to derive income directly, but to open the door to future hedging business; however, unless this business is assured, the time expended should be covered by a sales charge. This helps prevent any perception of a conflict of interest by the survey provider.

VIII. (4) The treasurer, or someone operating in that capacity, and the broker or outside service provider certainly can contribute to a management team. Senior management must be represented, whether by the president, chief financial officer, or some other executive. The team serves to develop the management program and to give the company oversight capability.

IX. Hedge losses can be unacceptable if they are unexpected. Managers and department heads may be more tolerant of such losses if they understand them, have been allowed prior input, and are kept informed as members of a management team.

X. (2) Education is the most valuable contribution of a knowledgeable advisor, especially during the development phase of a ongoing currency management program.

XI. The most important considerations of an information management system are: (1) what information needs to be reported and to whom, (2) who needs to report it, (3) how often it should be reported, and (4) how it will be transmitted.

XII. (4) A basic requirement of an information management system is hedge accounting, or a method of matching hedges with exposed positions. Account balances should be updated on a daily basis and the hedge should be liquidated immediately if it is no longer offsetting an exposure.

XIII. (4) Policy should stipulate that the program be consistent with corporate objectives, remain within stated risk parameters, and be transparent (fully disclosed). Policy should also require that the program be cost effective, operate within the limitations of available resources, and be stress tested regularly.

XIV. (4) An effective hedge model is a pre-determined plan of action within acceptable risk parameters which furthers the goals and objectives of the company.

XV. (2) An appropriate hedge in this case would be a classic 100% hedge. 100% of the exposure is hedged 100% of the time. This model keeps the probability of both opportunity gain and market loss to an absolute minimum; therefore, the expected margin remains locked in place.

XVI. (2) In this case, the classic 100% hedge would be the least appropriate because it precludes any chance of gain from exchange rate changes. A possibility of gain must play a part in any program that is expected to increase—and not just protect—profitability. Of course, the program may not be profitable, but loss-producing instead. The tolerance for market risk must be high enough to allow for this possibility.

XVII. (3) Transparency, as defined here, means that all aspects of a currency management program are fully disclosed and understood by corporate management. To achieve this, "plain vanilla" derivatives may be a requirement for one company but not another, depending on the degree of expertise involved. Illiquid positions, such as currency swaps, may be taken as long as management recognizes and accepts the resulting risk.

XVIII. (3) The cost/benefit analysis compares the benefits of the hedge with the costs, including transaction costs. The potential cost of the hedge burden would not be a factor because that cannot be determined in advance.

XIX. (2) Operations risk is the most common cause of major financial loss in hedge programs. This risk refers to the lack of, or break down of, controls on trading procedures. This may result in unreported losses accruing because of error, undisclosed speculation, or hedging techniques being misapplied due to lack of knowledge.

XX. (4) Credit risk pertains to the potential of a hedge position producing a loss because the counterparty is financially unable to fulfill its obligations.

XXI. (1) *Do not over-leverage*, (3) *update price charts daily*, and (4) *do not liquidate simply to cut a loss* are three trading rules that are well suited for any type of hedging program. Note that the last rule (#4) is the opposite of the speculative trading rule to always cut losses quickly. Rule (#2), *always follow the trend*, may apply to certain hedge models but not to others; therefore, it is not a general rule of hedging.

Chapter Seven

I. Consultative selling strives to achieve a situation in which:

    1. The buyer wins and the seller loses
    2. The seller wins and the buyer loses
    3. The seller and buyer both win
    4. Neither party wins, but the company benefits

II. Prospect for currency management business only when:

    1. There is a chance for immediate compensation
    2. The prospect will pay for a foreign exchange survey
    3. You are assured that futures will be part of the program
    4. There is an opportunity for a long-term client/consultant relationship

III. In consultative selling, your most important sale is:

    1. Your credibility
    2. The financial strength of your firm
    3. A competitive commission structure
    4. Your firm's research capability

IV. Before your first appointment, you should know all you can about:

    1. Your product or service
    2. The prospect's exposure
    3. The prospect's operation
    4. All of the above

V. The best way to build credibility with a prospect is by:

    1. Achieving a highly developed product knowledge base
    2. Fully disclosing all material facts

3. Proposing personal benefits to the company

4. Correctly identifying all buying influences

VI. During a presentation, technical jargon should be kept to a minimum because:

1. Technical analysis is not very predictive

2. Chart patterns can rapidly change

3. It is difficult to understand

4. All of the above

VII. The *single buyer* theory implies that:

1. Only one person has the authority to buy any given thing at any one time

2. Buying decisions can be influenced only by one person

3. Only a single buyer is authorized to commit the company financially

4. The buyers must always benefit on an individual basis

VIII. In any given sales situation, the buyer wins when:

1. The company wins
2. The features have been fully recognized
3. A personal benefit has been obtained
4. He or she foresees higher bonus payments

IX. Usually the most important buying influence during your initial contact is the:

1. Coach

2. Treasurer

3. Chief Executive Officer

4. Economic buyer

X. Before the company is committed to your program, it must be approved by the:

1. Chief Financial Officer
2. Economic buyer
3. Technical buyer
4. Chief Executive Officer

XI. Match the buying influence with its most probable "win":

1. Coach	New opportunity
2. Chief Financial Officer	Financial solutions
3. Chief Operating Officer	Increased performance
4. Chief Executive Officer	Your success

Answers to Chapter Seven

I.   (3) Consultative selling strives for a win-win situation between buyer and seller. Anything less is economically indefensible or unethical. The only way to prospect for currency management business is with a consultative selling approach.

II. (4) The only way to justify the time, effort, and often the delayed compensation involved in prospecting for currency hedging business is when the objective is a long-term business relationship.

III. (1) Unless credibility is first established, nothing else offered will be of interest to the prospect.

IV. (4) You should be prepared to answer fully all questions regarding your product or service, and to ask *relevant* questions regarding the company's operation and exposures. The more you know in advance about the company, the more relevant your questions, and the more credible you are.

V.   (2) Anything *less* than full disclosure of all material facts is construed as unethical business practice or fraudulent. This includes omissions of facts as well as misleading statements. A sales presentation that is less than forthright quickly undermines any credibility of the presenter.

VI. (3) The probability of a presentation's being too technical is much greater than of its being too basic. Those of us in the financial industry all too often fail to recognize this fact. A presenter who talks over the heads of the audience is often considered arrogant and the speech intimidating. A speaker rarely gets a second chance to redeem himself.

VII. (1) At any given time, only one person within a corporation is authorized to make a specific buying decision concerning a specific product on any specific occasion. This "authority" may be (a) formally recognized; as with the role of purchasing agent; (b) informally recognized; i.e., the decision is of no great import and is made by whoever is available; (c) unrecognized, such as when power shifts occur because of office politics.

VIII. (3) The "win" in a win-win situation always involves a personal benefit for the buyer. This may or may not be the same benefit enjoyed by the company as a whole. A personal benefit satisfies someone on an emotional level, something a "feature" does not do.

IX.   (1) The most important buying influence at the initial stage of prospecting is the coach. This buyer helps smooth the way by opening doors, identifying other buyers, and identifying what might personally benefit them.

X.   (2) Only the economic buyer has the authority to commit the company financially. This is the buyer entrusted with the purse strings. It may be the CEO, a director, the major stockholder, or someone else.

XI.   (1) The coach attaches his star to yours and wins when you succeed; (2) The CFO seeks financial solutions more than anything else; (3) The COO is a user buyer who benefits personally by enhanced operating performance; (4) The CEO looks for new opportunities for the company.

Appendix II
Currency Exchanges
Worldwide

Country	Exchange	Currency	Eurorate
Belgium	Belgian Futures & Options Exchange (BELFOX)	US$/BF Exchange Rates (O)	BIBOR (F)
Brazil	Bolsa de Mercadorias & Futuros (BM&F)	US$ (commercial) (F,O) US$ (floating) (F,O) Flexible Currency (O)	one day and 30 day interbank deposits (F,O)
Chile	Santiago Stock Exchange	US$ (F)	
Denmark	FUTOP Market (Copenhagen Stock Exchange & FUTOP)		3-month CIBOR (F)
Finland	Finnish Options	US$/FIM (F,O)	3-month HELIBOR (Forward)
	Exchange, Ltd.	DM/FIM (F,O) SK/FIM (F,O) BP/FIM (F,O) DM/SK (F,O)	
	Helsinki Securities and Derivatives Exchange, Clearinghouse (HEX Ltd)	FRX Currency Derivatives (22 currencies) (F, O)	
France	March a Terme Int'l de France (MATIF)		3-month PIBOR (F, OF)
Germany	DTB Deutsche Terminbörse		1-3 month Euromark (F)
Hong Kong	Hong Kong Futures Exchange (HKFE)	Rolling Deutsche Mark (F) Rolling Japanese Yen (F) Rolling British Pound (F)	3-month HIBOR (F)

211

Country	Exchange	Currency	Eurorate
Hungary	Budapest Commodity Exchange	U.S. Dollar (F) Deutsche Mark (F) Japanese Yen (F) British Pound (F) Italian Lira (F) Swiss Franc (F) Czech Koruna (F) ECU (F)	1 & 3 month BUBOR (F)
	Budapest Stock Exchange	US$/HUF (F) Deutsche Mark (F) ECU/HUF (F)	1 & 3 month BUBOR (F)
Isreal	The Tel Aviv Stock Exchange (TASE)	U.S. Dollar Exchange rates (F,O)	
Japan	Tokyo Intn'l Financial Futures Exchange (TIFFE)	US$/JY (F)	3-month Euroyen (F, OF) 3-month Eurodollar (F) 1-year Euroyen (F)
Netherlands	Amsterdam Exchanges (AEX-Optiebeurs)	U.S. Dollar (F,O)	
	Financiele Termijnmarkt Amsterdam N.V. (FTA)	US$/ DG (F)	
Russia	Moscow Interbank Currency Exchange	U.S. Dollar (F)	
Singapore	Singapore International Monetary Exchange, Ltd (SIMEX)	Deferred Spot US$/JY (F) Deferred Spot US$/JY (F)	Euroyen (F,OF) Eurodollar (F,OF) Euromark (F,OF)
Spain	Meff Renta Fija (MEFF-RF)		90-day MIBOR (F,OF) 360-day MIBOR (F,OF)
Sweden	OM Stockholm AB (OMS)		STIBOR -FRA (F) HELIBOR -FRA (F)
United Kingdom	London International Financial Futures and		1 month Euromark (F) 3 month Euromark (F, OF)
	Options Exchange (LIFFE)		3 month Euroyen (F, OF) 3 month Euroswiss (F, OF) 3 month Eurolira (F,OF) 3 month Sterling (F,OF) 3 month ECU (F, OF)

Country	Exchange	Currency	Eurorate
United States	Chicago Mercantile Exchange (CME) IMM (div of CME)	Deutsche mark (F, OF) Canadian dollar (F, OF) Swiss franc (F, OF) British pound (F, OF)	LIBOR (F, OF) Eurodollar Time deposit (F,OF) 3 month Eurodollar (F, OF) Euroyen (F)
United States	Chicago Mercantile Exchange (CME) IMM (div of CME)	Japanese yen (F, OF) Australian dollar (F, OF) French franc (F, OF) DM/JY cross rate (F) BP/DM cross rate (F) BP rolling spot (F, OF) JY rolling spot (F) DM rolling spot (F, OF) DM currency forwards JY currency forwards	
	GEM (div of CME)	Mexican Peso (F, OF) Brazilian Dollar (F, OF) New Zealand Dollar (F, OF) South African Rand (F, OF)	
	MidAmerica Commodity Exchange (MidAm)	Australian Dollar (O) British pound (O) Canadian dollar (O) Deutsche mark (O) Japanese yen (O) Swiss franc (O)	Eurodollar (F)
	New York Cotton Exchange NYCE		
	FINEX (div of NYCE)	U.S. Dollar Index (F, OF) Sterling/D-Mark (F, OF) Sterling/Yen cross rate (F) Sterling/Swiss Franc (F) DM/Yen (F, OF) DM/Krona (F, OF) DM/French Franc (F, OF) DM/Italian Lira (F, OF) D-Mark/Swiss Franc (F,OF) D-Mark/Spanish Peseta (F) US$/British Pound (F, OF) US$/D-Mark (F, OF) US$/Yen (F, OF) US$/Swiss Franc (F, OF) US$/Canadian Dollar (F) US$/South African Rand (F)	

Country	Exchange	Currency	Eurorate
		Sterling/US$ (F, OF)	
		Australian Dollar/US$ (F)	
United		New Zealand Dollar/US$ (F)	
States			
	Philadelphia Stock Exchange (PHLX)		
	Philadelphia Board of Trade (PBOT)	British Pound (O, F)	
		Canadian Dollar (O, F)	
		Deutsche Mark (O, F)	
		Swiss franc (O, F)	
		French franc (O, F)	
		Japanese yen (O, F)	
		Australian dollar (O, F)	
		Spanish Peseta (O)	
		Italian Lira (O)	
		ECU (O,F)	
		DM/JY cross rate (O)	
		BP/DM cross rate (O)	

source: 1998 Source Book, Futures

Abbreviations

F	Futures
O	Options
OF	Options on Futures
BF	Belgian Franc
BP	British Pound
DM	Deutsche Mark
FIM	Finnish Markka
SK	Swedish Krona
HUF	Hungarian Forint
JY	Japanese Yen
DG	Dutch Guilder

The table includes a selection of currencies and Eurorates available on exchanges world wide. No representation is made as to the accuracy of this grouping, nor has any consideration been given to trading access or factors such as credit risk, political risk and liquidity. All risk factors should be thoroughly examined before utilizing any contract in a currency management program.

U.S. dollar contracts on foreign exchanges may be used to hedge the local currency of the country in which that exchange in located. For example, the U.S. dollar contracts on the Bolsa de Mercadorias y Futuros in Sao Paulo, Brazil, could be a market in which to hedge the Brazilian Real. Currencies also may be hedged indirectly. For example, the Swedish krona can be traded on the PHLX as a cross rate, or on the Finnish Options Exchange through the Finnish Markka, assuming sufficient liquidity.

Eurorates ending in 'IBOR' or 'BOR' refer to "Interbank Offered Rate." The first letter(s) refer to the city, usually the financial center of the home country of the currency quoted. For example, 'PIBOR' is the Paris Interbank Offered Rate for the French franc, or "Eurofranc." "MIBOR" is the Madrid Interbank Offered Rate for the Spanish Peseta, or "Europeseta." The exception is the London Interbank Offered Rate (LIBOR) which refers to the U.S. dollar, or Eurodollar.

Appendix III
World Value of the
Dollar

The table below is reprinted from editions of the Wall Street Journal published four years apart. A comparison of the two columns suggests the types of fiscal and monetary policies that influenced currency values within that time frame. We can see, for example, that the East Caribbean dollar, the Belize dollar, the Bahrain Dinar, and the Liberian dollar, to name a few, have not budged one penny, but remained firmly pegged to the U.S. dollar. (Changes in the real rate of exchange in these currencies are not revealed.) Other currencies show the effects of economies wracked by inflation. Afganistan, Algeria, Angola, Bulgaria, the Commonwealth of Independent States (Russia), Cuba, Ghana, Nigeria, Yemen and others have experienced currency devaluations of at least 50%. Some countries, Turkey, for example, appear stalked by true hyper-inflation.

Of course, like a corporate balance sheet, these value columns are simply snap shots of two specific dates, and tell us little about the historic events that produced them, or the the current events now taking place. Still, we can draw some conclusions. We can be sure, for example, that no currency starts out at 100,000 to the U.S. dollar; it takes a run-away printing press to depreciate values to that level. The picture changes daily. On November 7th, 1997, the entire block of Southeast Asian currencies, firmly pegged to the U.S. dollar just a few weeks earlier, were in the midst of a free fall to levels then still unknown, taking their nation's equity and debt markets with them.

COUNTRY (CURRENCY)[+]	VALUE 11/5/93	VALUE 11/7/97
Afghanistan (Afghani - c)	1050.0000	4750.0000
Albania (Lek)	110.0000	145.5500
Algeria (Dinar)	19.7700	56.7992
Andorra (Peseta)	135.8900	144.5350
Andorra (Franc)	5.9113	5.7281
Angola (New Kwanza - 16, 20)	6500.3200	257128.0000
Antigua (E Caribbean $)	2.7000	2.7000
Argentina (Peso)	0.9981	0.9998
Aruba (Florin)	1.7900	1.7900
Australia (Australian Dollar)	1.4852	1.4258
Austria (Schilling)	11.9485	12.1430
Bahamas (Dollar)	1.0000	1.0000
Bahrain (Dinar)	0.3770	0.3770
Bangladesh (Taka)	39.7505	45.0000
Barbados (Dollar)	2.0113	2.0113
Belgium (Franc)	36.3100	35.2900
Belize (Dollar)	2.0000	2.0000
Benin (C.F.A. Franc)	295.5650	572.8100
Bermuda (Dollar)	1.0000	1.0000
Bhutan (Ngultrum)	31.3700	36.5320
Bolivia (Boliviano - o)	4.3950	5.3200
Bolivia (Boliviano - f)	4.4000	5.3300
Botswana (Pula)	2.5374	3.7594
Bouvet Island (Norwegian Krone)	7.3715	6.9386
Brazil (Cruzeiro - c - 4,) Real, 21	183.5900	1.1077
Brunei (Dollar)	1.5940	1.5730
Bulgaria (Lev)	30.2120	1709.0000
Burkina Faso (C.F.A. Franc)	295.5650	572.8100
Burma (Kyat)	6.1868	6.2616
Burundi (Franc)	234.5430	350.7350
Cambodia (Riel)	3500.0000	3000.0000
Cameroon (C.F.A. Franc)	295.5650	572.8100
Canada (Dollar)	1.2948	1.4047
Cape Verde Isl. (Escudo)	74.2000	92.9500
Cayman Islands (Dollar)	0.8500	0.8282
Centrl African Rp (C.F.A. Franc)	295.5650	572.8100
Chad (C.F.A. Franc)	295.5650	572.8100

COUNTRY (CURRENCY)+	VALUE 11/5/93	VALUE 11/7/97
Chile (Peso - o)	444.3000	466.0200
Chile (Peso - m)	412.3000	418.7300
China (Renminbi Yuan)	5.7868	8.2817
Colombia (Peso - o - 3)	817.0100	1290.5000
Commwlth Ind Sts (Rouble - m)	1177.0000	5907.5000
Comoros (C.F.A. Franc) (22, Franc)	295.5650	429.6075
Congo, People Rp (C.F.A. Franc)	295.5650	572.8100
Costa Rica (Colon)	148.1000	240.9650
Cuba (Peso - 23)	1.3203	23.0000
Cyprus (Pound*)	1.9470	1.9825
Czech (Koruna - 8)	29.5560	32.7270
Denmark (Danish Krone)	6.7735	6.5098
Djibouti (Djibouti Franc)	178.1650	177.7200
Dominica (E Caribbean $)	2.7000	2.7000
Dominican Rep (Peso - d)	13.0000	14.5000
Ecuador (Sucre - d)		
Ecuador (Sucre - o)	1838.0000	4247.0000
Egypt (Pound)	3.3405	3.4015
El Salvador (Colon - d)	8.7100	8.7550
Equatorial Guinea (C.F.A.Franc)	295.5650	572.8100
Estonia (Kroon)	13.5300	13.6856
Ethiopia (Birr - o)	5.0000	6.6440
Faeroe Island (Danish Krone)	6.7735	6.5098
Falkland Island (Pound*)	1.4801	1.6881
Fiji (Dollar)	1.5360	1.4863
Finland (Markka)	5.7675	5.1524
France (Franc)	5.9113	5.7281
French Guiana (Franc)	5.9113	5.7281
French Pacific Isl. (C.F.P. Franc)	107.4781	104.1472
Gabon (C.F.A. Franc)	295.5650	572.8100
Gambia (Dollar) (Dalasi, 24)	9.4700	10.4573
Germany (Mark)	1.7000	1.7100
Ghana (Cedi)	705.0000	2230.0000
Gibraltar (Pound*)	1.4801	1.6881
Greece (Drachma)	243.0500	269.3100
Greenland (Danish Krone)	6.7735	6.5098
Grenada (E Caribbean $)	2.7000	2.7000
Guadeloupe (Franc)	5.9113	5.7281
Guam (U.S.$)	1.0000	1.0000

COUNTRY (CURRENCY)+	VALUE 11/5/93	VALUE 11/7/97
Guatemala (Quetzal)	5.8240	6.1929
Guinea Bissau (Peso) (CFA Franc, 25)	5000.0000	572.8100
Guinea Rep (Franc)	812.2900	1132.0000
Guyana (Dollar)	126.0000	142.8000
Haiti (Gourde)	12.0000	17.4131
Honduras Rep (Lempira - d)	6.9600	13.2050
Hong Kong (Dollar)	7.7275	7.7310
Hungary (Forint - 13)	99.3800	194.3400
Iceland (Krona - 6)	71.3400	70.7350
India (Rupee - m)	31.3700	36.5320
Indonesia (Rupiah)	2098.5000	3300.0000
Iran (Rial - o - 17)	1661.0000	3000.0000
Iraq (Dinar- o) (m, 26)	0.3125	1200.0000
Ireland (Punt* - 7)	1.3995	1.5117
Israel (New Shekel)	2.9408	3.5407
Italy (Lira)	1642.0000	1677.3500
Ivory Coast (C.F.A. Franc)	295.5650	572.8100
Jamaica (Dollar - o)	27.5000	34.5500
Japan (Yen)	108.2500	123.7800
Jordan (Dinar)	0.6850	0.7090
Kenya (Shilling)	68.5379	63.7500
Kiribati (Australia Dollar)	1.4852	1.4279
Korea, North (Won)	2.1500	2.2000
Korea, South (Won)	807.1000	980.3000
Kuwait (Dinar)	0.2992	0.3032
Laos, People DR (Kip)	720.0000	1310.0000
Latvia (Lat - 10)	0.6100	0.5785
Lebanon (Pound)	1713.5000	1530.5000
Lesotho (Maloti)	3.3672	4.8279
Liberia (Dollar)	1.0000	1.0000
Libya (Dinar)	0.3013	0.3835
Liechtenstein (Franc)	1.5045	1.3953
Lithuania (Litas - 11)	3.9500	4.0008
Luxembourg (Lux. Franc)	36.3100	35.2900
Macao (Pataca)	7.9825	7.9861
Madagascar DR (Franc)	1850.0000	4985.0000
Malawi (Kwacha)	4.4704	17.8750
Malaysia (Ringgit)	2.5625	3.2990
Maldive (Ruflyaa)	11.9750	11.7700

COUNTRY (CURRENCY)+	VALUE 11/5/93	VALUE 11/7/97
Mali Rep (C.F.A.Franc)	295.5650	572.8100
Malta (Lira*)	2.5542	2.6281
Martinique (Franc)	5.9113	5.7281
Mauritania (Ougulya)	113.8100	165.8450
Mauritius (Rupee)	18.4514	21.7150
Mexico (New Peso - 1)	3.1470	8.2900
Monaco (Franc)	5.9113	5.7281
Mongolia (Tugrik - o - 19)	400.0000	800.3200
Montserrat (E Caribbean $)	2.7000	2.7000
Morocco (Dirham)	9.3746	9.3887
Mozambique (Metical)	5053.0729	11495.0000
Namibia (Rand - c)	3.3672	4.8279
Nauru Islands (Australia Dollar)	1.4852	1.4279
Nepal (Rupee)	46.3772	56.9500
Netherlands (Guilder)	1.9067	1.9277
Netherlands Antilles (Guilder)	1.7900	1.7900
New Zealand (N.Z. Dollar)	1.7960	1.5958
Nicaragua (Gold Cordoba)	6.2438	9.8252
Niger Rep (C.F.A. Franc)	295.5650	572.8100
Nigeria (Naira - d, m)	35.0000	80.0200
Nigeria (Naira - o)	n.a.	21.8860
Norway (Norwegian Krone)	7.3715	6.9386
Oman, Sultanate of (Rial)	0.3850	0.3850
Pakistan (rupee - 18)	29.9000	44.0060
Panama (Balboa)	1.0000	1.0000
Papua N.G.(Kina)	0.9787	1.5279
Paraguay (Guarani - d)	1793.0000	2228.0000
Peru (New Sol - d)	2.1550	2.7125
Philippines (Peso)	27.5000	34.9750
Pitcairn Island (N.Z. Dollar)	1.7960	1.5958
Poland (Zloty - o, 27)	20619.0000	3.4730
Portugal (Escudo)	174.0500	174.6800
Puerto Rico (U.S.$)	1.0000	1.0000
Qatar (Riyal)	3.6400	3.6409
Republic of Macedonia (Denar)	n.a.	53.4285
Republic of Yemen (Dinar)	0.4609	n.a.
Republic of Yemen (Rial) (a, 28)	16.5000	124.0000
Republic of Yemen (Rial - o, 28)	18.0000	n.a.
Reunion, Ile de la (Franc)	5.9113	5.7281

COUNTRY (CURRENCY)+	VALUE 11/5/93	VALUE 11/7/97
Romania (Leu)	1055.5000	7791.0000
Rwanda (Franc)	146.4367	293.9000
Saint Christopher (E Caribbean $)	2.7000	2.7000
Saint Helena (Pound Sterling*)	1.4801	1.6881
Saint Lucia (E Caribbean $)	2.7000	2.7000
Saint Pierre (Franc)	5.9113	5.7281
Saint Vincent (E Caribbean $)	2.7000	2.7000
Samoa, American (U.S.$)	1.0000	1.0000
Samoa, Western (Tala)	2.5975	2.6609
San Marino (Lira)	1642.0000	1677.3500
Sao Tome & Principe (Dobra)	240.0000	2390.0000
Saudi Arabia (Riyal)	3.7506	3.7508
Senegal (C.F.A. Franc)	295.5650	572.8100
Seychelles (Rupee)	5.2604	5.0100
Sierra Leone (Leone)	550.0000	780.0000
Singapore (Dollar)	1.5940	1.5730
Slovak (Koruna - 9)	32.8150	33.3510
Slovenia (Totar)	127.4817	161.4235
Solomon Island (Solomon Dollar)	3.1807	3.7495
Somali Rep (Shilling - d)	2620.0000	2620.0000
South Africa (Rand - f)	4.3425	n.a.
South Africa (Rand - c)	3.3672	4.8279
Spain (Peseta)	135.8900	144.5350
Sri Lanka (Rupee)	49.0175	59.9250
Sudan Rep (Dinar)	13.0000	142.9000
Sudan Rep (Pound - c)	130.0000	1428.6000
Surinam (Guilder)	1.7850	401.0000
Swaziland (Lilangeni)	3.3672	4.8279
Sweden (Krona)	8.1600	7.4493
Switzerland (Franc)	1.5045	1.3953
Syria (Pound - d)	21.5000	41.8500
Taiwan (Dollar - o)	26.8500	30.9485
Tanzania (Shilling)	455.1372	614.5650
Thailand (Baht)	25.3500	38.5500
Togo, Rep (C.F.A. Franc)	295.5650	572.8100
Tongo Island (Pa'anga)	1.4852	1.3066
Trinidad & Tobago (Dollar - 2)	5.5200	6.1800
Tunisia (Dinar)	1.0065	1.1063
Turkey (Lira)	13499.5000	185237.0000

COUNTRY (CURRENCY)+	VALUE 11/5/93	VALUE 11/7/97
Turks & Caicos (U.S.$)	1.0000	1.0000
Tuvalu (Australia Dollar)	1.4852	1.4279
Uganda (Shilling - l)	1181.9231	1148.0000
Ukraine (Karbovanet - 12)	31000.0000	n.a.
Ukraine (Hryvnia - 29)	n.a.	1.8765
United Arab Emir (Dirham)	3.6710	3.6729
United Kingdom (Pound Sterling*)	1.4801	1.6881
Uruguay (Peso Uruguayo - m)	4.2400	9.9050
Vanuatu (Vatu)	122.5600	118.8800
Vatican City (Lira)	1642.0000	1677.3500
Venezuela (Bolivar - d - 30)	101.0000	498.8000
Vietnam (Dong - o)	10785.0000	12206.0000
Virgin Is, Br (U.S.$)	1.0000	1.0000
Virgin Is, US (U.S.$)	1.0000	1.0000
Yugoslavia (New Dinar - 14) (31)	105.0000	5.6895
Zaire Rep (Zaire - 15)	3.5100	117500.0000
Zambia (Kwacha)	350.0234	1360.0000
Zimbabwe (Dollar)	6.7913	13.4500

*U.S. dollars per National Currency unit.

+(a) Free market cental bank rate.
(b) Floating rate.
(c) Commercial rate.
(d) Free market rate.
(e) Controlled.
(f) Financial rate.
(g) Preferential rate.
(h) Nonessential imports.
(i) Floating tourist rate.
(j) Public transaction rate
(k) Agricultural products.
(l) Priority rate.
(m) Market rate.
(n) Essential imports.
(o) Official rate.
(p) Exports.
(n.a.) Not available.

Notes: Novemeber 5, 1993

⁺(1) Mexico, 1 January 1993: New currency called the New Peso introduced.
(2) Trinidad and Tobago, 13 April 1993: floating exchange rate.
(3) Colombia, 20 May 1993: Peso revised definition.
(4) Brazil, 3 August 1993: New currency called the Cruzeiro Real introduced.
(5) Uruguay, 1 March 1993: New currency called the Peso Uruguayo
     introduced.
(6) Iceland, 27 June 1993: Krona devalued by approx 7.5%.
(7) Irish Rep., 30 January 1993: Punt devalued by approx 10%.
(8) Czech, 1 January 1993: County now split into two republics Czech and
     Slovak.
(9) Slovak, 10 July 1993: Koruna devalued by approx 10%.
(10) Latvia, 3 September 1993: Rates now being quoted for Latvia.
(11) Lithuania, 21 July 1993: Exchange rates now being quoted for Lithuania.
(12) Ukraine, 19 August 1993: Karbovanet devalued by approx 68.66%.
(13) Hungary, 30 September 1993: Forint devalued by approx 4.5%.
(14) Yugoslavia, 1 October 1993: Rate as of 8-20-93. Rate no longer available.
(15) Zaire Rep., 3 November 1993: New currency called New Zaire
     introduced.
(16) Angola, 13 October 1993: Kwanza devalued by approx 38.46%.
(17) Iran, 14 April 1993: Rial devalued by approx 7%, currency now
     convertible.
(18) Pakistan, 22 July 1993: Rupee devalued by approx 5.7%.
(19) Mongolia, 27 May 1993: Tugrik devalued by approx 62.5%.

Notes: November 7, 1997

(20) Readjusted Kwanza.
(21) New currency.
(22) New currency.
(23) Specific rate for FX houses only.
(24) New name.
(25) Replaces peso.
(26) Official rate abolished 1/96.
(27) New denomination.
(28) Official rate abolished 1/96.
(29) New currency.
(30) Devalued approx 41% 12/95.
(31) New denomination.

Source: Bank of America Global Trading, London. Adapted from the *Wall Street Journal*, November 8, 1993 and November 10, 1997.

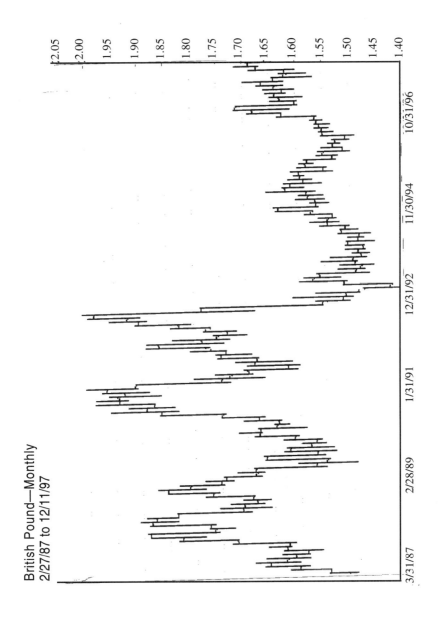

British Pound—Monthly
2/27/87 to 12/11/97

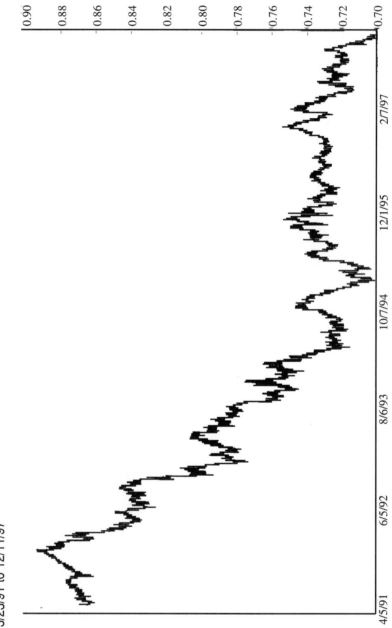

Canadian Dollar—Weekly
3/23/91 to 12/11/97

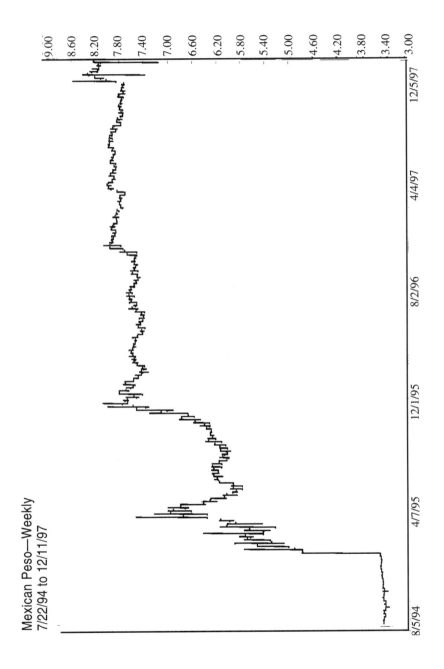

Mexican Peso—Weekly
7/22/94 to 12/11/97

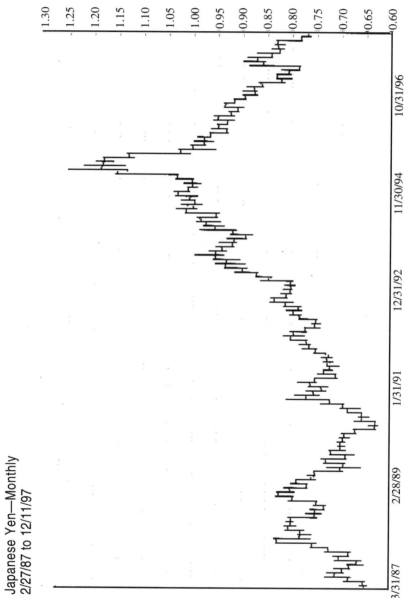

Japanese Yen—Monthly
2/27/87 to 12/11/97

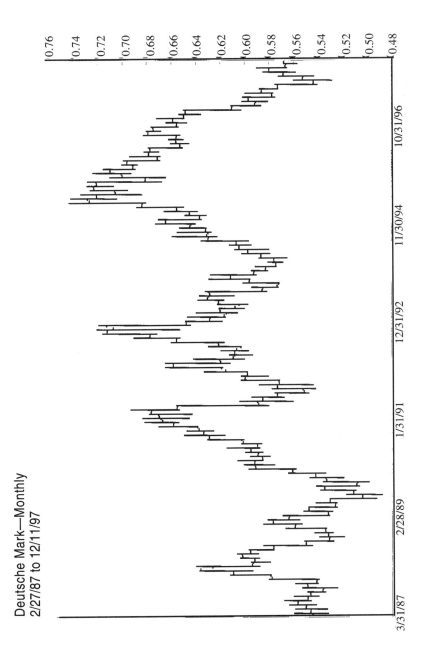

Deutsche Mark—Monthly
2/27/87 to 12/11/97

End Notes

Notes from Preface

1. Knut Engelmann, Reuters Online, January 3, 1998
2. "Capital Flow Sustainability and Speculative Currency Attacks,"
    Research Department Staff, Finance & Development (Washington
    D.C., International Monetary Fund) December 1997:8-9
3. Gary Shoup, *The International Guide to Foreign Currency
    Management*, 1st Ed., (Grove City, PA: The Center for Futures
    Education) 1995, 60

Notes from Introduction

1. Stephen O. Morrell, "Trends in the Market for Derivatives,"
    Derivatives Risk Management Service, edited by G. Timothy
    Haight (Boston, Mass: Warren, Gorham   & Lamont, 1996): 1B-3
2. Mary Ann Burns editor., "Interview: Chicago Exchange Leaders
    Confront Challenges," *Futures Industry*, vol. 3, no. 2 (March/April
    1993): 22

Notes from Chapter 1, An Overview

1. Gregory J. Millman, *The Floating Battlefield: Corporate Strategy in
    the Currency Wars*, New York, New York: AMACOM, 1990).
2. Editorial, "Getting Around the 'S' Word," *Futures*, No. 14
    (December 1992): 8.
3. Millman, *The Floating Battlefield*.
4. Editiorial Staff, "Selling Risk Management Concepts,"
    from"Politics of Risk," *Corporate Risk Management*, Vol. I, No. 1,
    (September/October 1989): 8

Notes from Chapter 2, The Competitive Edge

1. James W. Slentz, A*n Introduction to Interbank Foreign Exchange and Rolling Spot*, (Chicago, IL: Chicago Mercantile Exchange, 1993). Mr. Slentz is Senior Director, Risk Management Applications, Marketing Division, Chicago Mercantile Exchange.

Notes from Chapter 3, Basic Concepts of Foreign Exchange

1. John Stuart Mill, *Principles of Political Economy*, Vol. II; (New York, NY: D. Appleton and Co. 1864): 23.
2. Neil Wallace, "Why Markets in Foreign Exchange are Different from Other Markets," *Quarterly Review* (Federal Reserve Bank of Minneapolis), Winter, 1990: 12-18.
3. Hans M. Flickenschild and Martin G. Gilman, "Developments in International Exchange and Payments Systems," *World Economic and Financial Surveys* (Washington, DC: International Monetary Fund, 1992): 5. Hans Flickenschild and Martin Gilman directed a staff team from the Exchange and Trade Relations Department, IMF, in the research and presentation of this survey.
4. Flickenschild and Gilman, 18.

Notes from Chapter 4, Basic Concepts of Hedging—None

Notes from Chapter 5, Foreign Currency Exposure

1. Boris Antl, "Accounting Exposure," *Management of Currency Risk*, Vol. 1 (London, England:Euromoney Publications PLC, 1989): 25-27.

Notes from Chapter 6, The Currency Management Program

1. Editorial Staff, "Selling Risk Management Concepts" from "Politics of Risk," *Corporate Risk Management*, Vol. 1, No. 1, (September/October 1989): 8.

Notes from Chapter 7, Prospecting the Corporate Client

1. Robert B. Miller & Stephen E. Heiman, *Strategic Selling* (New York, NY: Warner Books, Inc., March 1986): 69-99.
2. Miller & Heiman, 122-123.

Index